Costa Brava

Barcelona and the Coastal Resorts

Jarrold Publishing

CONTENTS

Tossa de Mar

This is the Costa Brava

Perhaps you have already decided where your dream holiday will be spent, or you may already be there, relaxed and stretched out on some golden beach with this little book in your hand. On the other hand you may not yet have made up your mind, or perhaps the members of the family cannot agree. Whichever it is, do please feel that this invitation is directed to you. For this travel guide should tell you everything you might wish to know about the Costa Brava and the Costa Daurada and, indeed, everything you ought to know if you want to get as much as possible out of your holiday; everything about this 250-km-long strip of coast in north-east Spain, which, during recent years, has developed in a most astonishing way into one of the favourite holiday venues in Europe.

However, it is not really so surprising, for the two coasts we are talking about offer so much variety that they are tailor-made for what we now expect from a holiday — the sun glowing in a cloudless sky to warm and tan you (and burn you if you are not careful!), bathing beaches full of hustle and bustle, a real holiday pleasure-ground and a visual feast for those who like to see all there is to be seen, but also remote, wildly romantic or idyllic bays with quiet spots for those who prefer the pleasure of their own company or that of a friend, where the day passes like a dream. Large seaside resorts with well known names for the international set seeking adventure, as well as little fishing villages where modern life has yet to intrude. All this is linked by the crystal-clear, blue or turquoise waters of the Mediterranean, warm and pleasant, the water from which life itself comes and which has once again become the elixir of life to countless people who seek refreshment, relaxation and renewed strength.

The 'Wild Coast'

The strip of coast between Portbou on the French border and Tarragona in the south provides a surprising and almost inexhaustible variety. The Costa Brava — the 'Wild Coast', which, geographically speaking, begins at Roussillon in France — lives up to its name in so many places. In the north, where the foothills of the Pyrenees sweep down to the sea, it is cruel and aloof; on the peninsula of Cap de Creus and Cadaqués, solemn and melancholy. Between L'Escala and L'Estartit it is completely inaccessible; between Sant Feliu and Tossa, on the other hand, highly dramatic. It becomes mild and gentle as it sinks into the sea on the Gulf of Roses, idyllic in the bays at Begur and Palafrugell, romantic between Tossa and Lloret, and it provides wide beaches at Platja d'Aro, Lloret and Blanes.

The 'Golden Coast'

South of Blanes it joins the Costa Daurada — the 'Golden Coast'. While this cannot compare with the Costa Brava for variety and exciting beauty, it surpasses it for flat beaches and places to bathe. The coastline is now much less rugged and the mountains have receded. The towns and villages are arrayed like a necklace of pearls along the road to Barcelona, to the south of which lie the towns of Castelldefels and Sitges with their glittering attractions. The coastal area dealt with in this guide ends at historic Tarragona.

Catalonia

The two coastlines are joined under the heading 'the Catalonian Coast', for the countryside in which you wish to spend your holiday is called Catalonia and the people whom you will meet there are, in the majority at least, Catalans. Catalonia is the name given to the country in the north-east of the Iberian Peninsula, between the Pyrenees, the Mediterranean and the mouth of the Ebro. It can look back on a unique history which is identical only in part with the history of Spain itself, and the Catalans speak their own language, which they are anxious to retain. (See 'Phases of History', page 11.) The Catalans, almost 4 million in number, are spread over the

Blanes market

Lemons growing in the Costa Brava region

provinces of Girona, Barcelona, Lleida and Tarragona, and their capital is Barcelona.

> Some place names have differing spellings in Castilian ('high' Spanish) and Catalan. As this book deals mainly with Catalonia, we have used the Catalan names throughout. A list showing both Spanish and Catalan spellings will be found on page 94.

Catalonia is a well blessed land, more fertile, prosperous and progressive than most other areas of Spain. The sun does not burn down as mercilessly as it does further south; the climatic contrasts are not as marked as, for example, in the Castilian highlands, and the winters are mild and mostly damp. The raw winds are held back by the Pyrenees; only on the coasts does the *Tramontana*, a cutting north wind, sometimes blow in winter. The vegetation is comparatively lush — you can see it particularly well from the air — and the green of the cork-oaks and pine forests is the predominant colour. Beeches, chestnuts and fir trees also grow in the mountain valleys.

The Harvest of Land and Sea

Catalonia has a varied and developed agriculture. Wine and olives, almonds and hazel-nuts all produce good harvests; rice is grown among the flat coastal lowlands, tobacco in the hills, and the cultivation of vegetables, flowers and grain also plays an important part. The tractor has almost completely replaced the mule on the farms. He can still be seen, as innocent as a lamb and patient as ever, standing, just for decorative purposes, in the welcome shade of the house wall, laden with ceramic goods for tourists.

On the other hand, fishing on the Catalan coast is declining. Unfortunately, it must be said that to a large extent the Mediterranean has been fished out. The modest catch which the fishermen will land at your holiday resort is scarcely enough for their own needs. Yet, thanks to its advantageous position and to the enterprising spirit of its inhabitants, who have always been industrious seafarers and merchants, Catalonia has developed into the largest and most important industrial region of Spain.

The Catalan way of life

No wonder then that the Catalans have a certain self-assurance, and rightly so. Basically, they are convinced that Spain could not manage without them, but they could well do without Spain. Their relationship with the central state, as created and administered by Madrid, is somewhat fragile. They stand aloof and react most sensitively to any imagined or real attempt to make their decisions for them, or to attacks on their privileges or independence.

In contrast to the Castilian, the Catalan is more enterprising, modern in approach, down-to-earth and industrious. It has been said that, of the famous figures in Spanish literature created by the great Cervantes, Don Quixote, with his high ideals, sense of honour and strict morals, represents the pure embodiment of the Castilian, while his shrewd companion Sancho Panza must have been a Catalan.

Meeting the People

You may perhaps at this moment be relaxing on the beach, doing nothing in particular. However, it is well worth while going out and meeting the people among whom you are spending your holiday. That is much easier here on the Catalan coast than it is in some other holiday centres where tourism has to a large extent killed the original style of living and the rhythm of life as handed down through generations. Just go quietly into one of the fishing inns where tourists do not normally go because the menu is not in English, drink what the others are drinking and try the delicious *tapas* (see page 18). In that way you will quickly make contact with the locals without any problem, even if there are language difficulties. The Catalan is generally open-minded and interested and does not just view the tourist as a curiosity or someone to be 'ripped off'; his sound self-awareness guards against that. It can quite easily happen that you will find yourself accepted into a group of people who will take the greatest pleasure in offering you a little something; if so, don't be mean when it is your turn!

There are other ways in which the special nature of the Catalans can definitely influence your holiday pleasure. It can safely be said that Catalan enterprise and business sense make themselves particularly noticeable in the tourist sphere, and most agreeably so. That great Spanish magic word *mañana* — meaning tomorrow, the day after or not at all — plays a far lesser role in Catalonia than in other parts of

Las Ramblas, Barcelona

Spain. As seen by the north Europeans the Catalans — if we can be permitted such a generalisation — are a happy mixture of 'Latin' and 'moderate' characteristics. Anyone who has only a limited time for his holidays knows how much it means if he can rely on a promise or arrangement, if the service in the hotel is good (and it is often remarkably good), if — and this is actually true in most of Spain — he does not have to worry about being overcharged. Certainly, the Catalans will not provide you with that great, wanderlust type of adventure. If that is what you are seeking, you would do better to cycle through Turkey or join a camel caravan in the Sahara. For those in need of a rest and seeking a normal holiday, however, the Catalan coasts are undoubtedly very worth while.

Essential details in brief

Name: España (Spain).

Founded: 1479, by the marriage of the heirs of Aragón and Castile.

Form of Government: Constitutional monarchy based on a parliamentary democracy. Head of state: King Juan Carlos I. The state parliament consists of two chambers, the *Congreso* with 350 members and the *Senado* with 253 senators. Both are elected for four years. The present constitution came into force on December 7th 1978. Since autumn 1982 the Socialist Party (PSOE) has ruled with an absolute majority.

Administration: 17 autonomous regions.

Flag: Horizontal stripes: red-yellow-red.

Languages: In addition to the official state language of Spanish (Castilian), the following languages enjoy equal rights: on the east coast in Catalonia, Catalan (about 24% of the population of Spain), Basque in the Basque country, and Galician (akin to Portuguese) in Galicia in the north-west.

Religion: Almost exclusively Roman Catholic.

Population: 38 million inhabitants (U.K. 57 million). 76 inhabitants per sq. km (U.K. 235).

Capital: Madrid (about 5 million inhabitants).

Territory: 504,811 sq. km (just over twice as large as the U.K.), divided as follows: the mainland 492,265 sq. km, the Balearics 5014 sq. km, the Canary Islands 7500 sq. km, Ceuta and Melilla and four more coastal possessions in North Morocco 32 sq. km.

Tourism: In 1984 the total number of people who crossed the border into Spain was 43 million, 80% of whom were tourists.

Mineral resources: Iron, copper, lead, manganese, tin, zinc, potash and coal.

Important Exports: Agricultural products (fruit, oil, wine), motor cars (especially Ford and other foreign makes), steel, shoes, cement.

Vital Imports: Crude oil, meat, maize, oil seed and machinery.

Time: Central European Time, plus one hour in the summer.

Highly decorated architecture of the Sagrada Familia, Barcelona

Phases of History

The first historical traces in the area which we now call Catalonia were left behind by the Iberians. They were related to the Berbers, and came from North Africa. At present an Iberian settlement is being excavated in the area between Torroella de Montgrí and Palafrugell. Remains of Iberian ceramics found there are evidence of the age-old tradition of ceramic production in Catalonia. Between 700 and 500 B.C. Celtic tribes came over the Pyrenees towards the south and mingled with the Iberians.

As early as the middle of the 6th c. Greek merchants founded the settlement of Emporion (Empúries, see page 34) on the Gulf of Roses.

The Romans

Around 200 B.C. the Romans began to gain a foothold in Spain, after they had defeated the Carthaginians and driven them out. Yet it was only later, under Julius Caesar, that they succeeded in incorporating the Iberian peninsula into the Roman Empire. In the period which followed, it became so thoroughly Latinised that even Roman emperors, such as Trajan and Hadrian, and great Roman intellectuals, including the poet Martial and the philosopher Seneca, could come from Spain. Much evidence still remains of the period of Roman rule, in the shape of walls, bridges, cisterns, aqueducts and baths, in Tarragona and Empúries in particular, as well as in Barcelona.

The Roman Empire in Spain collapsed under the onslaught of the Germanic hordes. In the year A.D. 414 the Visigoths, under their king Ataulf, conquered Barcelona and temporarily made it their headquarters. There is still no better explanation of the origin of the word Catalonia than that it is merely an alteration of 'Gotalania', i.e. the land of the Goths. With the Germanic peoples Christianity also gained a foothold in Spain.

The Moors

In the long term, the event with the most significant consequences in the history of Spain was the invasion by the Arab Moors in the 8th c. In the north of Spain their rule lasted only 90 years, whereas Toledo remained Moorish for 500 years and Granada for almost 800 years. We cannot dwell here on the powerful influence of the Moors on the cultural and artistic history of Spain. However, nobody doubts that the marked difference in mentality between the central and southern Spaniards on the one hand, and the northern Spaniards and Catalans on the other, is also attributable to the different lengths of time for which they were occupied.

The true history of Catalonia begins with the reconquest of Barcelona by the

Pont del Diable

Franks under Louis the Pious in the year A.D. 801. The counts of Barcelona, who were appointed by the Franks as a protection against the Moors, made themselves independent after a short time, and soon extended the Catalan lands down as far as Valencia, and out as far as the Balearics.

Aragón

In the year 1134 the Count of Barcelona married the heiress to the throne of neighbouring Aragón. The dynasty of the 'Kings of Aragón and Princes of Barcelona' became a great Mediterranean power, whose influence extended through southern France and Sardinia to Italy, Sicily and Greece. In the course of this development, the royal seat and port of Barcelona became a serious rival to the dominant maritime powers of Genoa and Venice. The Maritime Law, which was formulated in Barcelona in 1258, received international recognition. It was during this period, too, that many important historical monuments were erected, such as the cathedrals in Tarragona (see page 84), Barcelona (see page 68) and Girona (see page 54), as well as large parts of the famous *Barri Gòtic* in Barcelona. The progressive thinking of the time is also illustrated by the fact that Barcelona was the first Spanish city into which the art of book-printing was introduced.

Towards the end of the 15th c. two important events of world history changed the whole political scene in Spain. Firstly, in the year 1469 Ferdinand of Aragón-Catalonia married the heiress to the throne of Castile, Isabella. This marriage of the two most powerful dynasties in Spain was the foundation-stone upon which the national state of Spain was built. Madrid became the capital and seat of government. Barcelona was now just one of several royal seats of merely secondary importance. The other event was the discovery of America by Columbus in 1492, which led to the downgrading of Catalonia to a province. Spain's military and economic energies were now concentrated entirely on the new continent, and the Atlantic ports of Seville and Cádiz took over from Barcelona, which played no part in the trade with America. Moreover, the Mediterranean, once the centre of the known world, became little more than an inland sea of minor importance.

The times which followed brought little benefit to Catalonia. Eventually, the Catalans felt so neglected by Madrid that in the middle of the 17th c. they sought an alliance with France. However, this venture turned out very badly for them. Amongst other things, the University of Barcelona, founded in 1450, was closed. Gradually, Catalonia lost all its former *fueros* (privileges).

The cultural life of Catalonia did not escape the political and economic decline. Its language, Catalan, slipped more and more into obscurity, and, since there was a lack of both money and creative ideas, one may search in vain for important historical monuments from the Renaissance and Baroque periods, in which the rest of Spain is so rich. Many Catalans emigrated to America, as they saw no future in their own country.

The Catalan Revival

In the second half of the 18th c. Catalonia was at last allowed to trade with America. The resultant economic revival was interrupted at the beginning of the 19th c. by the invasion of Napoleon's armies, against which the people of the whole of Spain, but especially those of Catalonia, fought like heroes. When the first Spanish constitution was promulgated in Cádiz in 1812 the Catalans lost the last of their freedoms.

In the course of the 19th c. nationalism grew in Catalonia, its aims being to regain independence or at least extensive autonomy within a federal framework. The permanent result has been the revival of the Catalan language, a subject on which no true Catalan can speak without pride. Catalan, which is no nearer to Spanish than, say, French or Portuguese, is today the colloquial language which is understood everywhere in the country and is spoken beyond the boundaries of Catalonia itself, in Valencia, on the Balearics, in French Roussillon and in part of Sardinia. Since the educated sections of the community did not exclude themselves from this popular movement, it was even able to develop its own Catalan literature, the greatest pioneer and internationally best-known representative of which was Jacint Verdaguer (1845–1902).

Prophets in Tarragona Cathedral

During the Spanish Civil War (1936–39) separatist tendencies still flickered in Catalonia. However, with General Franco came long years of dictatorship, ending with his death in 1975. Now all the efforts of the Catalans are directed at becoming universally independent. In the spring of 1980 they attained economic and cultural autonomy within the structure of the young Spanish democracy.

Enjoying your holiday

Perhaps we take it too much for granted that we can go almost anywhere in the world at any time, to spend our holidays in the way we think best. Of course, there are certain restrictions: in some countries tourists are not very welcome at the moment; the money will not (yet!) quite stretch to Rio de Janeiro or Acapulco; and possibly our employer has been unreasonable enough to go on holiday just when we wanted to go ourselves.

However, we know well enough that we live in an age which opens up possibilities for us which people scarcely dared to dream about a few decades ago. Economic and social conditions now permit a large number of people to take several weeks' holiday in the sunny south. Open borders between states are accompanied by facilities for comfortable and time-saving travel, well regulated and safe conditions at the resort and a peaceful and friendly environment. Comfortable accommodation and civilised mealtimes and many more facilities are there for the asking.

Why mention all this? Quite simply because it can help us to get much more out of our holiday. The art of living and travelling is not just to take things for granted, but consciously to enjoy them, and in that way to double or even treble your holiday enjoyment — for the same money!

This psychological fine-tuning, so to speak, seems to be essential in order to ensure that a holiday fulfils one's expectations, namely, to have a truly enjoyable time. Then everything else will just evolve, provided, of course, that you have chosen the right place for your holiday.

Something for everybody

Now, of course, there is no fixed recipe for having a good time which will suit everybody. We all have different expectations, based on our personal preferences and conditions at home. If you come from the hectic, noisy bustle of a big city, then perhaps your idea of a good time is to be cut off from the world in a lonely bay, with just the lapping of the waves and the tangy aroma of the sea for company. The quiet-living small-town dweller, on the other hand, has possibly been waiting a whole year for the time when he can 'let his hair down' at last. Anyone who is ruled day in and day out by the conveyor belt or appointments diary may well want nothing more from his holiday than to idle away the days without a fixed plan, or simply to drift around and do nothing except whatever appeals on the spur of the moment. Although the actual recipe may differ according to the individual concerned, having a good and enjoyable holiday means finding a counterbalance to the daily round at home — in a word, 'relaxation'. Relaxation means doing things on holiday — they need not cost a penny — which we cannot do at home: living it up at night and having three-hour siestas, going for a walk along the beach at five in the morning, playing with the children or learning to dance the *sardana*, going on an excursion into the surrounding countryside to see the sights, compiling a four-course menu of fish specialities, swimming as far as you can every day or stretching your legs in a café while you watch the world go by . . . relaxation means enjoying the day and building up your energy for the all-too-early return to work.

The visitor who does this will certainly get his or her money's worth on the Costa Brava or Costa Daurada. Of course, 'one man's meat is another man's poison', so we will only touch on the various interests, leaving you to form your own judgements.

Left: Lovely guest-houses everywhere on the Costa Brava. Right: Ready for a sightseeing trip

Food and Drink

If you are a guest in a hotel on the Catalan coast you will normally have no cause to complain about the food, the generous quantities and the service. You may possibly find breakfast a bit meagre — as it is in all Latin countries. As regards the milky coffee which will probably be served at breakfast — if this is not to your taste you can either provide your own instant coffee or stick to tea.

At the main mealtimes, however, the first impression will be one of surprising sumptuousness. This is even more true of the midday meal (*almuerzo*) than the evening meal (*cena*). A normal Spanish meal generally consists of at least four courses:

1. Hors d'oeuvres (*entremeses*), salad or soup;
2. A fish, rice or noodle dish;
3. Meat, poultry or game with potatoes and vegetables;
4. Dessert (*postre*) with a sweet, ice cream, stewed or fresh fruit.

This is more than some stomachs can manage, especially as Spanish cooking is mainly based on olive oil which, although very digestible, does take a little time to get accustomed to. In any case, the maxim 'waste not, want not' not only betrays a certain lack of good manners, but is also not exactly free of risk when on holiday, for it can mean that you will be obliged to spend a day or two of your holiday in bed. In view of the limited appetite of many guests, some hotels should be commended for offering the choice of a glass of fruit juice as a starter.

Each place setting will have two glasses, one for wine and one for water. (Always order mineral water, even if it is not exactly cheap.) Wine and water are not mixed in Spain, as a light wine is drunk with meals. The most sensible thing is always to ask for the wine of the region (*ví de la casa, ví del país* — in Catalan, you always drink *ví* instead of *vino*), which will not be served in the bottle, but already poured out. While the Spaniards prefer white wine or rosé with food, most North European stomachs find that red wine (*ví negre*) goes better with the oily cooking.

To be honest it must be said that in the coastal hotels, although the meals will be 'Spanish', as far as the number of courses, the drinks and the late mealtimes are concerned, you will get only a hint of Spanish or even Catalan cooking. When you see the mixture of British, French, Dutch and German guests, you cannot really blame the hoteliers for going over to 'international cooking', which one takes to mean the most colourless and unoriginal dishes imaginable, because nowadays chicken, chops or fish portions fried until they are unrecognisable are less likely to be turned away than squid, octopus or a garlic sauce.

This is regrettable but under the circumstances not likely to change. However, when you are on holiday in a foreign country you should at least try their cooking, and tickle your palate with unfamiliar dishes, even at the risk of being disappointed. What the great gourmet Brillat-Savarin said in honour of the connoisseur — 'Discovering a new dish is more important for mankind than discovering a new star' — is also true, in principle, for those who go on a culinary voyage of discovery. So be brave enough to risk a tour of Catalan eating places (you will find a number listed under the individual towns and villages, but there are plenty of others worth a try); you will not regret it!

Quite understandably, the emphasis of Catalan cooking on the coasts is on the preparation of fish specialities and other seafood. The finest fish caught here is halibut (*mero*), served boiled, baked, roasted, in a sauce (*suquet*) and with rice. *Suquet de peix* is a stew, based on various recipes but always tasting good, made of different Mediterranean fish in a sauce of oil, tomatoes, onions, garlic and parsley. The Spanish variety of the excellent bouillabaisse, served here without stock, is called *zarzuela*, and a normal fish soup is *sopa de peix*.

Garlic

Apropos of garlic: it is used freely and often in Catalan cooking, just as it is in Provence. It reaches the ultimate in culinary refinement in *allioli*, a highly esteemed garlic mayonnaise adopted from Provence, and eaten with all kinds of meat, such as roast rabbit or lamb cutlets. You must make sure that it is freshly mixed, however. The esteem in which garlic is held is made clear in the observation of the southern Frenchman Marcel Boulestin: 'It is no exaggeration to state that, geographically speaking, peace and good fortune begin where garlic is used in cooking.'

Octopus

You will look in vain on the guest-house menu for the popular, but also misunderstood, octopus. However, every restaurant near the coast in Catalonia offers it, either cooked in breadcrumbs (*calamares a la romana*) or grilled (*a la*

planxa). Then there are the delicious shellfish, small and large prawns (*gambas, langostins*) and crayfish (*langosta*), best eaten a la planxa with a piquant sauce (*salesa romesco*) made of crushed shrimp-shells, garlic and paprika in oil. Other Catalan specialities are crayfish with chicken, and with snails; crayfish in chocolate sauce (*langosta a la catalana*) is not really to everyone's taste, although the more enterprising visitor might like to try it!

Paella

The truly representative and now internationally famous Spanish dish, however, is *paella valencia*, the richest and most mysterious dish that Spain has produced. Its secret lies in the fact that it allows unlimited varieties in practice — provided that the correct balance is retained as regards taste. Its basic ingredient is saffron-coloured glazed rice. To this are added chicken, pork, ham, sausage, crayfish tails, mussels, snails, eel and other fish, tomatoes, artichokes, peas, peppers, onions and garlic. The whole is cooked in a pan — paella means pan — over a wood fire.

Paella

Butifarra

You cannot avoid it; you simply must eat a paella before you go home. By rights the Spanish customs-officer should not allow anyone out of the country unless he can produce proof that he has tasted this world-famous speciality! Even if not all the ingredients listed above are included, you should be clear on one thing: a paella can lie very heavily on the stomach. If you do not wish to risk a disturbed night, you had better eat your paella for lunch rather than in the evening.

Farmhouse cooking

If you go a little distance away from the coast you will come across other Catalan specialities which are clearly of rustic origin. For example, stews (*puchero* or *escudella*) made of potatoes, chick-peas, chicken, sausage or beef are very popular. Chick-peas (*garbanzos*) or white beans (*judias*) are also served with the typical Catalan sausage, the *butifarra*. You really must try tomato bread with ham (*pa amb tomaquet i pernil*), a favourite in Catalonia, and a potato omelette (*truita espanyola*). This all sounds like real country cooking — and it certainly is.

Tomato bread with ham

Tapas

Very few of us really need two solid meals a day, even if we are travelling. However, in the bars you will find that splendid institution, *tapas*, delicious little tit bits,

Tapas

appetisingly spread out and inviting you to try them — olives, mussels, oysters, crab, small pieces of sausage, sardines and salad. In the town centres you can drift from bar to bar and taste the different specialities — a cheap and pleasant occupation. Even though tapas are basically considered appetisers, they will easily do instead of lunch if you do not feel like a sit-down meal. It is customary to drink one of the numerous aperitifs with your tapas, but probably the best thing to drink with the mainly spicy snacks is a beer, which is usually perfectly drinkable in Spain.

Coffee

The finish to any meal, big or small, should in any case be a cup of the excellent black coffee, known as *café solo* or *café expres*. If you prefer it with milk, ask for a *café tallat*.

Sangría

A refreshing drink in the evening, especially popular with tourists, is *sangría*, made from apricots, oranges and lemons with ice-cold red wine poured over them. A note of warning: anyone who does not keep a close check on his intake can easily wake up with a thick head the next morning!

Shopping

You can, of course, take home with you carved wooden figures of Don Quixote and Sancho Panza, a fur donkey with its red felt tongue hanging out, a Torero doll embroidered in gold, fake castanets and other cheap souvenirs.

If you decide you would like something that will not just lie around the house unused then Catalonia does not offer you a great choice. Nevertheless there are some things of charm and value, especially ceramic goods, which have a long tradition of skilled workmanship here. La Bisbal is a centre for the production of ceramics. It is not far inland from the coast and a trip there is well worth while for those who are keen on these things. Neat and attractive practical baskets can be bought cheaply anywhere along the coast. This also applies to the beautifully grained boxes, bowls, platters, etc., made of olive-wood.

As is well known, you can still buy leather goods more cheaply in Spain than in Great Britain. However, the quality and workmanship of the leather varies considerably, and if it is very cheap be on your guard. This may be acceptable in the case of certain fashion Spanish goods which do not have to last very long, but for style and fashion Spanish shoes and handbags do not compare with those from Italy.

As regards fashion there are boutiques everywhere in the larger coastal towns where you can buy exactly the same things as you would in Blackpool or anywhere else. You will certainly find a better selection in Barcelona, where a shopping trip in the old town is well worth while. Or you can wander through the *El Corte Inglés* department store on the Avenue Diagonal. There you will find something of everything, and the air-conditioning is far from unwelcome when the temperature outside is about 28°C.

Please do not run away with the idea that Spain is a treasure trove for valuable but cheap antiques. The professional antique dealers have already searched the country far more thoroughly than you will be able to do. Quite apart from that, the customs will have a word to say on the matter (see page 89).

Shopping in Barcelona

✂ Festivals and Events

It is practically impossible to stay longer than a week in Spain without being involved in a festival of some kind. The Spaniards — and the Catalans are happy to be included in this — derive more pleasure from festivals and celebrations than almost any other people. The Spanish calendar contains a large number of official holidays — too many in the opinion of those who are concerned about the economic progress of the country. The festivals celebrated in Catalonia during the summer months include Whit Monday, May 1st, St John the Baptist's Day (June 24th), the Assumption of the Virgin Mary (August 15th) and Diada (a patriotic Catalan feast day, September 11th).

Local festivals play an even more important part in the lives of the people. The *Semana Santa* of Seville in Easter week, the celebration in honour of *San Isidro* in Madrid in May, *San Fermines* in Pamplona with the famous (or infamous) driving of the bulls into the arena (July 7th) and the September week-long festival of *Nuestra Señora de la Merced* in Barcelona are known throughout the world, and have become important tourist attractions. Even the smallest village pays homage to its saint, on the day named after him, with its *Fiesta Mayor*. Then the houses, squares, streets and above all the churches are decorated with flowers, banners and garlands, and are alive with music. Often the fiesta is combined with an annual cattle market, and it usually goes on for two or three days. In any event, the crowning glory is always the firework display in the evening, and not only because of the visible effects, for above all it must fizz, crack and explode as loudly as possible. In most mountainous parts of Spain, the echo thrown back from the mountainside adds to the enjoyment of the fireworks.

The delight the Spaniards find in their festivals, linked to their unshakeable Catholic faith, is simply unlimited. This also applies to the tourists, because it is so infectious. It frequently happens that the foreign visitor mixes with the people, and enjoys himself like everybody else.

The Sardana

One cannot imagine a Catalan festival without the *sardana*. The sardana is *the* Catalan dance, an age-old round dance probably brought over from Greece. The dancers — their number is immaterial — form a circle, join hands and move to the melodies of the *cobla*, an orchestra composed of various wind instruments, flutes, a drum, a double bass and a trombone. The melodies to which they dance are unmistakable, with their

Catalan in festive costume

Sardanas

almost monotonous repetitions, not 'full of Spanish exhilaration' but rather with a very restrained passion. The pattern of the dance steps is very precisely laid down and they are repeated at set intervals. The movements are measured, the faces of the dancers very concentrated and pensive, almost peaceful, under the spell of the dance. The sardana is always danced in the open air in the town square or on the streets.

Strangers can join the circle of dancers, even if they do not know the steps. They will be made welcome, but little attention will be paid to them. A man must also make sure that he does not break into the circle where a woman is dancing on the right of a man.

Water sports

Golf

🚶 Sports and Games

It was some years ago in Tossa. For three whole weeks, a man lay on the beach from 10 in the morning until 6 in the evening and slept, on his stomach in the mornings, on his back in the afternoons. At midday on the last day of the third week his wife woke him. 'Henry, wake up! We have to go home!'

'What, already?' sighed Henry, and he got up and trotted back to the hotel behind his wife.

No doubt Henry returned splendidly refreshed from his holiday, even though he neither put as much as a toe in the water nor really 'did' anything else. Yet most of us need to be up and doing on holiday — a change from just being idle. The nearest place to achieve that, of course, is in the water.

On most of the beaches on the two coasts 'bathing' really means 'swimming'. When you enter the water the ground soon disappears from under your feet, and you will have to swim in order to get any further. However, the waters of the Mediterranean support you well, so that even average swimmers can romp about in the deep without worrying. Nevertheless, by no means are all the beaches suitable for non-swimmers and children. Please therefore pay careful attention to the details given in the descriptions of individual places! Unfortunately, there are still no lifeguards on the Catalan coasts.

The rocky coasts and clear water in particular make the Costa Brava an ideal place for underwater sport. Even equipped only with goggles and a snorkel you can discover an exciting and magic world under the surface, from which, having once discovered its beauties, you will find it hard to drag yourself away. The same goes, of course, for the true divers, who will find real underwater paradises with subterranean

Watching others can be enjoyable

caves, coral banks and sunken ships, off Cap de Creus, around the Illes Medes, near L'Estartit or by the steep coastline close to Begur. However, you should not dive alone. If you do not have sufficient experience and someone to accompany you you should join a diving club.

At most places along the coast, except the smaller bays, you can hire rowing boats or the more comfortable and popular pedaloes. Motor and sailing boats, on the other hand, are rarely obtainable. You can comfortably explore every corner of the rugged coast in your own inflatable dinghy.

Anglers can find numerous lovely places along the coast, where they are sure to be rewarded with at least a modest catch. Fishing in the early hours of the morning should be the most promising; this is when the fishing boats return, often bringing with them a shoal of tasty *lubinas*. Relatively abundant hunting grounds for river fishing are the lower reaches of the mountain rivers Ter and Llobregat, in which there are carp and eels. Fishing permits are required, but the issuing of official papers can be a lengthy business.

There is also a wide choice of sports and games available on land: mini-golf courses, bowling alleys, tennis courts and, above all, riding stables can be reached easily from almost all towns. Even the serious golfer need not miss out on his sport on the Catalan coasts: on the Costa Brava there is a course near Platja d'Aro and one in Pals with an international reputation, and on the Costa Daurada there is one in Sitges and another in Tarragona.

An Evening out

It is always good to know what to expect from your chosen holiday resort. So it should be made quite clear that the Catalan coastal resorts are not particularly suitable for those who retire early to bed. Above all there are climatic reasons for this. After the incessant midday heat, when it is best to take a nap, the world does not come to life again until late in the afternoon, and reaches its high point in the final hours of the day. The squares and the streets in the towns, the cafés and bars are never fuller than they are between 10 p.m. and midnight. The evening stroll, the *paseo,* has always played a very important part in the social and business life of the Spaniard.

Visitors from abroad have quickly and readily adapted to this daily rhythm. There is obviously something in the Spanish air which makes them ask after the late evening meal, with a new-found spirit of adventure, 'Now what shall we do?'

The resorts on the Costa Brava and Costa Daurada have the answer. There is no shortage of diversions and amusements, and places such as Calella de la Costa or Lloret de Mar have raised evening entertainment to a fine art.

To meet the needs of the high proportion of young and youthful visitors, discothèques, 'beat clubs' and night clubs have sprung up like mushrooms everywhere. Some demand an admission fee, it is true, but in return they offer a programme with dance performances, in which the flamenco plays the main role. This dance comes from southern Andalusia and really has no right in Catalonia at all. However, it is now Spanish folk-music's most successful export, and the rhythmic precision of good flamenco dancers is a truly impressive experience which you should not miss at any cost.

The more romantically inclined will stay on the beach and listen to the true Catalan folk-music, the traditional fishermen's songs — the *habaneras,* or in Catalan *havaneres* — which have been sung more and more in the last few years. At the same time a typical *cremat* (a rum drink) will be brewed on an open fire; definitely a tremendous holiday experience!

More 'up-market' are the night-time excursions into the hinterland, where inns in the rustic Catalan style invite you to hours of convivial wine-drinking by candle-light. Many places also arrange barbecue evenings in the open air, with roast sucking pig or other delicacies.

Seafood spread

Hints for your holiday

Etiquette for the visitor

When in Rome (or rather Spain!) . . . etc. This is always a good rule, based on common sense as well as politeness. By following this you will certainly avoid much unpleasantness and misunderstanding. Moral standards in Spain have relaxed somewhat as far as dress is concerned. While the bikini and topless sunbathing have become accepted as a matter of course on the beaches, nude bathing is still not favoured and can sometimes lead to a fine. There are, however, some official nudist beaches.

However, what is allowed on the beach is still not acceptable in the town or the village. It is best to dress as though you were walking around town at home. Men dressed in shorts in Barcelona or Girona are not especially popular with the Spaniards. Be particularly careful to dress correctly when visiting churches.

Spanish men are very susceptible to feminine beauty. If you, ladies, should hear something said by a man which sounds like a compliment, just take this *piropo* calmly and continue on your way without batting an eyelid.

Spain is a polite country. *Por favor* — please — and *muchas gracias* — thank you — are indispensable words for foreigners.

The Spaniard is generous and will probably offer the person next to him a cigarette or invite him to have a drink. As a stranger you should return the compliment.

Drunks are seldom seen in Spain, and almost never in Catalonia. If you do see one, then it is not a Catalan. Spaniards simply fail to understand the need to drink oneself into a stupor and then make an exhibition of oneself.

Where to go and what to see

Costa Brava: the Empordà coast

Strictly speaking, the Costa Brava actually starts in France — near Argèles in Roussillon, where the great sandy arc of the Golfe du Lion ends and where the coast becomes hilly and rugged. Only the political boundary-line cuts across the geographical, geological and — as we have already seen — linguistic unity of the region. Collioure, Port-Vendres and Banyuls are, essentially, typical Costa Brava places. However, this holiday guide will concern itself only with the (considerably bigger) Spanish section of the Costa Brava, the northern part of which is also named the 'Empordà Coast' after the ancient town of Empúries.

The main direction of the Empordà coast is north to south. However, it follows such an adventurous and inconsistent route that, for example, L'Escala faces north, L'Estartit south, Roses south-west and El Port de la Selva north-west. The whole of the Empordà coast is not yet as developed as the southern part of the Costa Brava, and in certain places it is for all practical purposes completely inaccessible.

Cadaqués, Costa Brava

Portbou Pop. 2500

A typical rather dreary and unattractive border town, Portbou's most important feature is the railway station, where most travellers have to change, because of the wider rail gauge used in Spain. However, a few international expresses with adjustable bogies do run through from France to Barcelona. Even though Portbou has a small pebble beach and adequate accommodation facilities, it is not a very suitable holiday base.

Colera Pop. 400

The fishing and farming village of Colera has a 200-m-long beach of large pebbles and a few small bays. People travelling through are glad to stop off here for a swim. However, it has little to offer as a holiday centre. South of Colera there are more pretty bays which those touring by car may like to visit. The best known are Platja de Garbet and Platja de Grifeu, which also offers a particular attraction: on the bottom of the bay lies a sunken galley which can be seen distinctly when the water is clear, and is popular with divers.

Llançà Pop. 3000

The fishing port of Llançà is beginning to develop into a popular seaside resort. Swimmers mix with fisherfolk on the 400-m-long beach of coarse sand; fishing plays quite an important role here. Things worth seeing in Llançà are the fortified tower on the Romanesque church and the defensive wall.

El Port de la Selva Pop. 700

This is the old harbour of the town of La Selva de Mar, which is situated a few kilometres from the coast and has become relatively unimportant. The fishing village lies well protected in a west-facing bay, which is almost like a lake. A beach of fine, clean sand with shallow water makes the bay very suitable for a holiday with children. El

Port de la Selva is still one of the most typical places on the Costa Brava. Small bays such as Tamarina, Fornells, El Golfet and Cala Taballera are particularly pretty.

In the mountains above El Port de la Selva stand the ruins of the Benedictine monastery of *Sant Pere de Rodes* (Spanish: San Pedro de Roda) which are well worth seeing. From there you have one of the most beautiful views along the coast (see page 34).

Between El Port de la Selva in the north and Roses in the south, a peninsula juts out into the sea; its eastern end, Cap de Creus, is also the most easterly point on the Spanish mainland. Cadaqués and Portlligat also lie on the peninsula (see below). A journey through the peninsula is very impressive, going perhaps from El Port de la Selva to Cadaqués and then on to Roses, returning via Palau-Saverdera and Vilajuïga. The narrow but well surfaced mountain roads lead through a wilderness of lofty solitude, broken here and there by unexpected views of the shining blue sea below. Great expanses of stony rock-face are relieved only occasionally by a deserted courtyard or an olive grove, the whole crowned, unfortunately, by an American radar station, which appears almost surrealistic in a seemingly unreal lunar landscape.

Perhaps even more attractive is the sea trip around the peninsula, a good way of returning from Roses via Cadaqués to El Port de la Selva if you went by bus instead of taking your car. (You can, of course, equally well start the round trip from Roses and Cadaqués.) The coast of the peninsula is very rugged and varied, sometimes sombre, slate-grey and melancholy, especially around Cap de Creus, and sometimes majestic; and hidden bays offer a friendly invitation to swim.

Cadaqués Pop. 1500

Cadaqués was, for hundreds of years, a fishing village completely cut off from the hinterland and accessible only by sea. More recently, it has been connected by a road with Roses and El Port de la Selva. It lies on a bay fringed by rocks and cliffs, and with its whitewashed houses and narrow streets, and its church dominating the whole, it presents a picture of austere charm. With the unexpected severity of its shapes and colours, and its barren nature caused by exposure to the strong winds, it reminds one of the Cyclades island of Mykonos in the eastern Mediterranean. Many artists find inspiration here. Cadaqués, while not perhaps the most beautiful, is certainly one of the most interesting places on the Costa Brava. In a naval battle off Cadaqués in 1285, a French fleet was repulsed by a Catalan fleet. Because of its exposed position, the town was subject to constant attacks by foreign powers (French, Turkish, British). Completely dependent on the

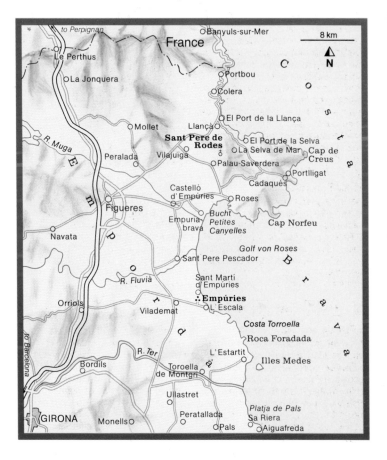

sea, the inhabitants of Cadaqués traded with America on their own initiative.

In the church stands a magnificent and lavishly appointed Baroque altar dating from the 17th c., the only one on the Costa Brava, which was spared from the wave of destruction during the Civil War in the thirties. Although Cadaqués enjoys an increasing influx of visitors, it has retained its originality, as characterised by its many art galleries, testimony to the artists who have worked there.

In August an international music festival is held here, in collaboration with famous artistes.

In the remote coastal area near Cap de Creus there is a colony of the Club Méditerranée which specialises in diving and all kinds of water sport.

 The beach at the main bay is narrow and stony. There is no lack of nice rocky bathing places nearby. However, they are not really suitable for smaller children.

 Ideal spot, especially around Cap de Creus.

 Rowing boats for hire.

 Some discothèques.

 One night club.

 In August there is an international festival of classical music.

 There are charming walks to be had along the coast in the direction of Cap de Creus. In the opposite direction a bridle-way leads to Roses via Cap Norfeu. Although in parts even the most resourceful of walkers will find it hard to trace, it is a walk of several hours through extraordinarily impressive country.

 In *Portlligat,* very near to Cadaqués, stands the house of

the painter, the late Salvador Dali. Anyone who knows Dali's pictures will recognise certain shapes, colours and motifs all around. A trip to the famous Dali Museum in Figueres is recommended.

Roses Pop. 9200

Situated at the southern end of the peninsula of Cap de Creus, on the magnificent sweep of the beautifully curved Golf de Roses. The hotel quarter of Roses adjoins the busy fishing harbour.

Roses was colonised even in Greek and Roman times. The new Roses grew up in the 11th c. and belonged to the county of Empordà. In the 17th and 18th c. the town was occupied several times by the French, who destroyed the old monastery and fortifications in 1795.

Roses is a very lively place; every day at six in the evening there is a fish auction in the fish hall. Each Sunday morning is market day. You should not miss either of these events.

Cadaqués on the Empordà coast

To the south, adjoining the hotel district and Roses beach, the big water-sports centre of *Empuria-Brava* has come into being, a purpose-built and well planned holiday complex for sailing and motor-boating. There are a modern marina and boatyard, shopping centres and public utilities, restaurants, a hotel, other sports centres and a private airport, all connected by canals by which those who own holiday homes can gain access to them by boat: all in all, an impressive attempt to plan for the holiday and amusement needs of the future.

Virtually unlimited, wide beach of fine sand falling away gently into the sea; very suitable for children.

 S Yacht hire.

 Rowing boats for hire on the beach.

Various children's playgrounds; bumper cars and trampolines.

Two riding stables with instructors and opportunities to go out for rides.

Water-skiing school in the neighbouring bay of *Petites Canyelles*.

In the bay of *Petites Canyelles*.

6 discothèques.

Fiesta Mayor from August 15th–20th.

2 night clubs with flamenco performances.

El Bulli (fish specialities, luxury category).

Very beautiful coastal trips by coach or boat from Roses to Empúries (see page 34), L'Escala (see page 32) and L'Estartit (see page 33). Coach trips to Girona, Figueres with the famous Dali Museum, Andorra and the Peralada gambling casino.

Continuing south the road passes through the flat and fertile region at the mouth of the rivers Muga and Fluvià. The principal crop here is rice. First of all the road leads away from the coast, and takes you to:

Castelló d'Empúries Pop. 2500

(9 km from Roses). At one time the capital of Empúries, Castelló d'Empúries declined in importance when the Muga silted up and ships could no longer reach the town. Today Castelló d'Empúries is a quiet little market town, but with some interesting reminders of its former glory:

The *Gothic cathedral* (13th–15th c.) with its three aisles and massive Romanesque clock tower; the former Stock Exchange (*Llotja*), also dating from Gothic times, which today serves as a town hall; and finally a daringly constructed 14th c. bridge over the Riu Muga.

At Castelló d'Empúries the road turns south again, through the flat, partly marshy coastal region of the Golf de Roses. This is the preserve of the rice and vegetable farmers, and of river anglers. From the point of view of tourism the area is little developed and in fact scarcely worth developing. With one exception:

Sant Pere Pescador

9 km from Castilló d'Empúries is a small holiday centre where camping enthusiasts can get good value for money.

 Club Nautico on the Fluvià river.

 Wind-surfing school.

 Fata Morgana, one of the most modern discothèques on the coast.

At Vilademat (11 km from Sant Pere Pescador) the road turns off towards L'Escala and Empúries.

L'Escala Pop. 3500

Lying at the southern end of the Golf de Roses but facing north, L'Escala is often at the mercy of the cutting Tramontana winds. The houses are not whitewashed (as they are in all other coastal places), so that the salt winds will not eat away at them. L'Escala is one of the most important fishing harbours on the Costa Brava; some would say the most important.

 In spite of an increasing number of summer visitors, L'Escala remains one of the most picturesque places on the Costa Brava. Here there still prevails the atmosphere of a fishing village with its own rhythm of daily life, something which is becoming increasingly rare on the Mediterranean.

 The beach here is not suitable for bathing. However, there are some lovely bathing places both towards Empúries and in the bays of Cala Riells, Cala Clota and Cala Montgó in the L'Estartit direction, with flat beaches very suitable for children.

 6 discothèques.

 Miriam, Roser 2 (both with fish specialities).

 You can take a long and charming walk along the wild and rugged coast to L'Estartit (4–5 hours).

There are both land and sea routes between the two coastal towns of L'Escala and L'Estartit, the one very pretty, the other highly dramatic. From L'Escala and Empúries a well surfaced road leads through hilly countryside.

Very soon you can see the massive castle above Torroella de Montgrí, some 15 km away.

Torroella de Montgrí Pop. 5500

This is an old, small town with a beautiful town hall square, a Gothic church (15th c.) and an imposing Renaissance palace, the *Palacio Marqués de Robert.* The town is dominated by the mighty castle, visible from afar, the *Castilló de Montgrí,* begun on the orders of King Jaime II. Only the external walls were completed, however, together with the cylindrical towers at each corner. The castle, from which there is a splendid view, is accessible only on foot (1 hour). It is a further 7 km from Torroella de Montgrí to L'Estartit.

The sea route from L'Escala to L'Estartit takes you along one of the wildest sections of the Costa Brava coast, the so-called Costa Torroella. As well as remote bays, which can be reached only by boat, there are also caves in which smugglers of yore could safely hide their wares, and the famous rocky cliff, the *Roca Foradada,* through which only small ships can pass. Nobody can say they really know the Costa Brava unless they have experienced the view from the sea around the Cap de Creus, or between Sant Feliu de Guixols and Tossa, in all its glorious splendour.

L'Estartit Pop. 1500

Formerly only a simple fishing village, in recent years L'Estartit has witnessed an astonishing transformation into a holiday resort. Its position on the broad sweep at the south end of the bay, with a wide beach, is scenically beautiful and favours all kinds of holiday activities. An extensive yachting marina offers protection from the Tramontana winds to sailing and motor boats. Ideal for all kinds of water sports.

L'Estartit is ideally suited to children.

8-km-long beach, wide, flat, with fine sand, particularly good for children and non-swimmers.

Sailing boats for hire, sailing school.

Very interesting diving around the *Illes Medes*; diving club.

Rowing boats for hire.

2 riding stables, excursions on horseback to the Riu Ter, and night riding.

Water-skiing school.

River fishing (seldom possible on the Costa Brava) in the Riu Ter; very popular.

International golf course.

Cycles can be hired locally. They are in great demand for trips inland.

Children's playground with round-abouts.

Catalan restaurant in *Camp Torre Gran* (exclusive).

5 discothèques.

3 night clubs.

Fiesta Mayor from July 16th to 26th, with sea procession, fishing competition and sardana.

Long and charming walks along the wild and rugged coast to L'Escala (4–5 hours).

There are excursions by boat to the north, along one of the wildest sections of the Costa Brava coast, and to the south, to the romantic bays of Sa

Riera, Aiguablava and Tamariu. In smaller boats you can sail to the off-shore group of islands, the Illes Medes, and to the rocky tunnel named *Roca Foradada*. Glass-bottomed boats are a particular attraction.

 The Hinterland

It is well worth making long or short trips inland from all the places on the Empordà coast. Josep Pla, one of the great Catalan authors, wrote: 'How many people have found that, only a few kilometres from the coast, a different world begins, with a discreet charm, where time goes more slowly!'

Follow this advice and find out how relaxing and impressive it can be to discover something new, away from the hustle and bustle of the beach.

Sant Pere de Rodes

In the mountainous hinterland behind El Port de la Selva stand the splendidly impressive ruins of what was once the massive Benedictine monastery of Sant Pere de Rodes. The origin of the monastery has never been unearthed; however, it was described as 'very old' in a document as long ago as the year 943. The legend naming Charlemagne as the founder, therefore, is unlikely to be true.

During the whole of the Middle Ages the monks of Sant Pere de Rodes held absolute sway over the surrounding district, fished and grew olives, but also completely stripped the forests. In the culinary sphere, they are credited with having imported into Catalonia *allioli*, the world-famous garlic mayonnaise. In any event, the liking of the monks for that condiment is recorded in old monastery documents. The monastery church is Romanesque and was consecrated in the year 1022. In the 18th c. the monks, having grown weary of the solitary life, left their refuge, which was then completely plundered by the valley-dwellers. There still remains a labyrinth of deserted halls, corridors and cells, in an impressively dominant situation 600 m up on the slope of the Sierra de Roda, and with a magnificent view as far as France and also over the Empordà coastal region in the south.

From El Port de la Selva it is a one-hour climb on foot to the monastery, and this is best undertaken early in the morning. You can, however, take the car to Vilajuïga, which is easily reached from Llançà or Roses. From Vilajuïga there is a good road nearly all the way up to the monastery (visiting times in summer 9 a.m.–2 p.m. and 4–8 p.m.)

Not far from Sant Pere de Rodes — 15 minutes on foot — lies the castle of *Sant Salvador*, built by the counts of Empúries. According to legend the Holy Grail was kept here. The view from the castle is very beautiful.

Empúries

The most interesting and venerable historic site on the Costa Brava is Empúries, the ancient Emporion. The extensive area of ruins, which so far have been only partly excavated and explored, lies on the Golf de Roses in the immediate vicinity of the fishing and seaside resort of L'Escala. Shortly before you enter the town a road goes off to the left to the small village of Sant Martí d'Empúries, 2 km away. From here you can obtain an informative preliminary view over the whole site.

About the middle of the 6th c. B.C., Greeks from Phokis in Asia Minor founded a settlement here. It can be assumed that these were the same merchants who had earlier founded the Greek settlement of Massilia (Marseilles), in order to trade with the Gauls — as they did here with the Celto-Iberians. They chose a small island between the mouths of the rivers Fluvià and Ter. The water surrounding this island, like that in its harbour, has dried up over the centuries. The island was situated where the houses of the village

Empúries

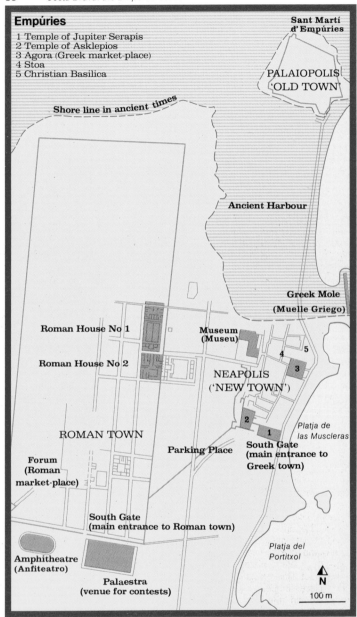

Empúries

1 Temple of Jupiter Serapis
2 Temple of Asklepios
3 Agora (Greek market-place)
4 Stoa
5 Christian Basilica

Sant Martí
d'Empúries

PALAIOPOLIS
'OLD TOWN'

Shore line in ancient times

Ancient Harbour

Greek Mole
(Muelle Griego)

Roman House No 1

Museum
(Museu)

Roman House No 2

4   5

3

NEAPOLIS
('NEW TOWN')

2   1

Platja de
las Muscleras

ROMAN TOWN

Parking Place

South Gate
(main entrance to
Greek town)

Forum
(Roman
market-place)

South Gate
(main entrance to Roman town)

Platja del
Portitxol

Amphitheatre
(Anfiteatro)

Palaestra
(venue for contests)

N

100 m

of Sant Martí now stand, above the ruins of the Palaeopolis (old city) which have been buried by drifting sands. In the year 540 Phokis in Asia Minor was destroyed by the Persians. The exiled inhabitants of the town fled across the Mediterranean and sought refuge in the 'colonies' founded by their countrymen. As the little island was beginning to get too small for them, the Greek settlers moved over to the mainland and founded a new city, the Neapolis. It was given the name Emporion, under which it is repeatedly mentioned in ancient literature by Cato and Livy.

From small beginnings Emporion developed into a flourishing commercial centre and soon became the most important Greek base on the Iberian Peninsula, indeed in the whole of the western Mediterranean. Strong cultural influences also spread from here all over western Europe. The old Iberian settlement of Indica, west of the Neapolis, and the Greek city grew together over the centuries.

The most important monuments which have survived from the time of the Greeks are the south gate, once the main entrance to the city, with massive cyclopean walls, the Asklepios Temple and the Stoa, a temple-like building of which only small remains can now be seen.

During the second Punic War against the Carthaginians the city was conquered by the Romans under Scipio the Elder (209 B.C.). They extended the harbour to be their base in the western Mediterranean. Later the centre of Euporion was moved to the west of the Neapolis, where the Iberian settlement of Indica had once stood. A further new city was built here for the veterans of the legions who had fought under Caesar in Spain. Its situation and ground plan are known, but little excavation has yet taken place. Emporion grew ten-fold under Roman rule, and became the largest Roman city in Spain. The Neapolis, however, became less and less important, and was finally deserted completely by its inhabitants.

The most important Roman buildings to be seen are: the Temple of Jupiter Serapis in the Neapolis, the Forum, the Amphitheatre, the South Gate and two elegant Roman houses with stucco and mosaic decor in the 'Roman Town'. The whole 400-m-length of the 5-m-high south wall has also been exposed. Empúries Museum is in the Neapolis. It houses many of the sculptures found here, stucco-work, mosaics, ceramics and everyday articles. Some, however, are only copies; the originals including the Asklepios statue can be seen in the archaeological museums of Barcelona and Girona.

In the Christian era, Emporion gradually lost its leading role to Tarragona. It is true that the Visigoths made it the see of one of their bishops, but even that could not prevent its decline. Emporion was finally finished off by the Normans. During one of their attacks they laid it to waste so completely that during the next thousand years the drifting sands inexorably buried it. Excavations were not begun until the early years of this century. By far the greater part of this site still awaits the archaeologists' spades.

Excursions with guides to Empúries-Emporion are regularly arranged from almost all the places along the Empordà coast.

Peralada

Peralada, with its casino, is a pretty place to aim for in the late afternoon or evening. In the summer months good concerts are often presented, ballet evenings are arranged and demonstrations of flamenco dancing are given. Any tourist office will provide details.

The rocky coast of the southern Costa Brava

Costa Brava: the Southern part

In the area between Begur and Blanes, the scenery of the Catalan coast shows its most attractive and benevolent side. The gently undulating hinterland displays rich fertility — the brown fields, the green meadows and pasture land, crowned by the shimmering, silvery glow of the olive groves. Near the coast the forests thicken, and pine and cork-oak trees — this being the centre of the cork industry — reach right down to the sea. Their dark green stands out against the rich ochre and red clay of the steep cliffs which disappear into the crystal-clear turquoise waters of the bays.

The Costa Brava is a landscape full of contrasts, romantic and idyllic, dramatic and primitive; the changing impressions follow one after the other. However, the most marked contrast of all, which has given this strip of coast its international reputation, has not yet been mentioned — fine scenery in one place and hustle and bustle in the next. For only a short distance behind the secluded bay we find the next big holiday resort, the meeting point for all those who do not like being on their own, and where night often becomes day. This is the place for anyone who really likes to 'live it up'.

Begur Alt. 220m, Pop. 2200
Begur is not right by the sea, but is a good starting-off point for visiting various particularly charming bays for swimming. As a result, it has developed into a tourist centre of some importance.

The picturesque town, set in a semi-circle around the castle mound, was founded in the 14th c., and from the very beginning was strongly fortified to protect it from countless raids by pirates. Typical are the arcaded balconies which embellish the houses of many of those who emigrated to America and returned home wealthy. The fortifications, especially some of the round towers,

Begur

have in part been well preserved. It will certainly be worth your while visiting the *castle ruins* on the top of the mountain. From here there is a magnificent view over the neighbouring coasts, the Bay of Pals, the Medes Islands and, when visibility is good, as far as the Pyrenees.

 Rowing boats for hire.

 Ideal spot for diving.

 Golf in *Platja de Pals*. 18 holes.

The following are within easy reach of Begur: *Sa Riera* (2 km), *Aiguafreda* and *San Tuna* (4–5 km), *Fornells* and *Aiguablava* (5 km).

Well worth while is a trip to the hotel *Parador de Aiguablava*. A path runs round the hotel from which you can look down on the coast and the unusually blue water (*aigua blava*).

Also very charming is the drive from Sa Riera to Platja de Pals, with a unique view of the Illes Medes.

Palafrugell Alt. 65 m, Pop. 15,000
Palafrugell is one of the largest towns on the Costa Brava. It lies 3 km from the

coast, and is the starting point and shopping centre for the resorts of Tamariu (4 km), Llafranc and Calella (each 3.5 km), which are also administratively linked with it. The town is a centre of the gradually diminishing cork industry.

The name Palafrugell appears for the first time in the 10th c. For a long time it belonged to the counts of Barcelona, and then to the canons of the monastery of Sana Ana in Barcelona.

Worth seeing is the 15th c. *parish church* with its Baroque altar. There is a market every Sunday where the farmers' wives offer their wares; a gloriously colourful country scene.

🍴   *Reig* (crustaceans and shellfish, paella), *Es Nius* (very typically Catalan).

✂   Fiesta Mayor from July 20th–22nd.

Tamariu Pop. 100

Tamariu lies on an idyllic bay surrounded by pine trees. Quite near is the secluded and still undeveloped bay of *Aiguaxellida*. Above it, a development of modern holiday homes is being built.

Nearby is the 250-m-deep cave *d'En Gispert*, through which you can pass in shallow-draught boats. Especially beautiful at sunrise.

🏠   Tamariu is an exceptionally quiet place.

🎣   Moray and conger eels.

⛱   Beach about 250 m wide of coarse sand is suitable for children.

⛵   Rowing boats for hire.

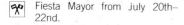

🔱   3 riding stables in *Calella de Palafrugell* (see entry).

🍴 🍴   *Reig* in Palafrugell (see entry).

🚶   Short walks along the coast, e.g. to Aiguablava or to the Sebastià lighthouse (see under Llafranc).

🚌   Frequent scheduled boat trips along the Costa Brava to Lloret or Blanes (3–4 hours). Opportunity to swim there. Return in the afternoon along the same route. Scenery is most rewarding.

Llafranc Pop. 400

Popular resort in a bay with a sandy beach some 500 m in length, and the marina of a Spanish water-sports club.

It was a Roman settlement, as is indicated by the remains of a temple below the present church. To the north-east rises the Cap de Sant Sebastià, on the top of which has been built a hermitage with a chapel (18th c.). This old refuge is a sprawling, rural building with a commanding view from its terrace. Not far away stands a lighthouse which casts its beam over a distance of 50 km.

🏠   Comparatively quiet place, without much night life.

⛱   The beach is relatively wide and suitable for children.

🏍   On the road to Palafrugell.

⛵   Rowing boats for hire.

🔱   3 riding stables in *Calella* (see entry).

🎣 🖼 🔍 ⛳ 🔦 ⛺

🍴   *Levante; Llafranc.*

✂ 🎸   *Fiesta Mayor de Santa Rosa,* with sardana and water games, on August 30th.

🚶   Pretty walk along the river bank to Calella; 1 hour to the lighthouse and the Sant Sebastià hermitage.

🚌   Scheduled boat trips along the Costa Brava to Lloret or Blanes

Calella de Palafrugell and Llafranc

(3-4 hours). Return in the afternoon along the same stretch. Scenery is most rewarding.

Calella de Palafrugell Pop. 350

This prettily situated former fishing village is a bustling resort, concentrated on one large and several small bays. Typical of Calella are the vestibules — *les voltes* — of many of the houses which look out over the fishing beach of Port Bo.

Calella — not to be confused with the bigger Calella de Mar in the province of Barcelona — was always the fishing port of Palafrugell. A park of extraordinary beauty, especially in spring, is the *Botanical Garden* on the slopes of Cap Roig, the southern extremity of the Bay of Calella. Guided tours through the garden are arranged from time to time.

Calella is the liveliest of the resorts around Palafrugell, but still relatively quiet compared with Platja d'Aro or Lloret.

Varied rocky and sandy beaches.

On the road to Palafrugell.

Foreign tourists can become temporary members of the *Poseidon* diving club.

 Rowing and motor boats for hire.

 3 riding stables with instructors and the possibility of going out for rides (some distance from the town).

 At various hotels.

 Els Rems (Catalan cuisine).

 Pretty path along the coast to the Botanical Garden, to Llafranc and on to Cap de Sant Sebastià.

Scheduled boat trips along the Costa Brava to Lloret or Blanes (3–4 hours). Bathing at midday. Return in the afternoon by the same route. Scenery is extremely fine.

Fish market in Palamós

Palamós Pop. 11,000 approx.

This is an old town of mixed fortunes which today is accessible to sea-going ships. The harbour, which faces west and is therefore particularly well protected, is important, especially as a fishing centre and for the export of cork. Brisk trade led to a notable degree of prosperity, which is reflected in the wealth of consumer products. In recent years, thanks to its long beach, Palamós has developed into a popular resort. Palamós was founded in 1277; in the year 1299 the Catalan fleet sailed from here to conquer Sicily. The town has always been subjected to strife and suffered in particular from repeated pirate attacks. In the year 1543 it was almost completely destroyed by the buccaneer Chaireddin Barbarossa.

Worth visiting are the 14th c. Gothic *parish church* with its Baroque chapel, added in the 18th c., and the museum, *Cau de la Costa Brava,* with its interesting collection of shells. The fish auction which takes place daily at the fish market is particularly entertaining to watch.

Being a commercial and shipping centre, Palamós is a very lively town, and has little to recommend it to anyone seeking peace and quiet. On the other hand, the *La Fosca* beach, which actually belongs to Palamós but is situated 2 km further north, is very much quieter.

Both the beach of Palamós itself (700 m long) and the smaller one at La Fosca (300 m) are of fine sand and gently sloping, very suitable for children.

S Yacht marina, sailing school.

Rowing and motor boats for hire.

 Maria de Cadaqués (fish specialities).

Platja d'Aro

🎵 Numerous cafés with dancing.

🍷 Flamenco dancing in the *Savoy*.

✂ Fiesta Mayor from June 24th–26th; July 16th seamen's festival in honour of the Virgen del Carmen.

🚶 You will find the scenery very beautiful, but the going somewhat arduous, if you walk as far as the small beaches and bays further north (2 hours from La Fosca to Cap de Planes).

Between Palamós and the Platja d'Aro (9 km) there is a varied and charming stretch of scenery with steep cliffs and a number of small bays and beaches. Sant Antoni de Calonge, within the boundaries of Palamós, and its 700-m-long beach, Comtat de Sant Jordi with some large hotels, and Platja d'Aro all merge into each other without any recognisable boundaries. Platja d'Aro, like S'Agaró and Santa Cristina d'Aro, belongs to the municipality of *Castell d'Aro* (Alt. 42 m, Pop. 1500) which lies 3 km from the coast and is of little interest to the tourist.

Platja d'Aro Pop. 1800

Platja d'Aro has developed very quickly into one of the most important and popular holiday resorts on the Costa Brava. With its fairly straight beach, nearly 2 km in length, and the streets running parallel to it, it is reminiscent of a resort on the Italian Adriatic. Beyond the two rocky peninsulas which enclose the beach are two similar but quieter bays, Sa Conca in the north and Platja Rovira in the south.

Platja d'Aro is a lively place with a lot of entertainment. It is less a question of

S'Agaró

peace and quiet here, more of activity.

 In *Santa Cristina*, 6 km inland (9 holes).

 The sandy beach is flat and slopes gently into the sea, so it is suitable for small children.

 10 tennis courts.

 Rowing boats for hire; motor and sailing boats for hire in *S'Agaró*.

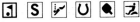

 Mas Sicars, a sophisticated café in the Catalan style with Catalan cooking; *Japet* (fish specialities).

 Many cafés with dancing, night clubs and discothèques.

 Big firework display on Mid-summer Day (St Juan, June 24th).

 Sardana every Tuesday.

 Pretty walks along the Mas Nou range of hills. Beach promenade in S'Agaró.

S'Agaró

3 km from Platja d'Aro is a place which is unequalled anywhere else on the Costa Brava, and in few places in Europe. However, it is available only to a limited degree to ordinary mortals. During the twenties and thirties on a small peninsula between Platja d'Aro and Sant Feliu de Guíxols were built the most exclusive summer residences in Spain. Planned and constructed as parts of a unified whole, the lavish villas and spacious gardens present a picture of well groomed luxury. Here in the high season will be found those from Barcelona who possess name, rank — and sufficient money! The focal point of society life is the luxury hotel, situated in

a great park and offering a whole galaxy of functions, ranging from festival events and grand balls to folk and other musical performances.

A wonderful coastal promenade, part of which is hewn out of the steep cliffs, and which is known as Camí de Ronda, allows the ordinary tourist to share in the enjoyment of the magnificent views from the peninsula, and at the same time to peep at the country houses of the well-to-do.

The beach at S'Agaró — also called Platja Sant Pol — is accessible to everyone.

 Rowing and motor boats for hire.

 Sailing boats for hire.

 Water-skiing school.

Sant Feliu de Guíxols Pop. 11,000

This town is known as the capital of the Costa Brava — a purely unofficial title. Like Palamós, Sant Feliu is a port rich in tradition, with a very good harbour which is in permanent but healthy competition with Palamós. With their prosperous economic life (cork industry, commerce, shipping) both towns are in any case closely related. Sant Feliu presents a shining example of the business activity and enterprising spirit of the Catalans. The normal meeting place is the prestigious marine promenade (*Passeig Marítim*) by the harbour. Apart from Lloret de Mar, Sant Feliu and Barcelona are the only places on the Costa Brava with bullfighting arenas.

The town gets its name from Saint Felix, who is said to have suffered a martyr's death here. (Girona also claims to be the place of his martyrdom.) Tradition says that the town was founded by Charlemagne. Under the protection of the Benedictine monastery, which ruled the district in the Middle Ages, the town flourished and soon possessed its

Vila Vella, a village from the middle ages at Tossa de Mar

own shipyards, stock exchange and maritime court. The inhabitants of Sant Feliu carried on a brisk trade with the Italian towns of Pisa and Genoa (which is why you can still detect an Italian influence on the townscape), and later also with America.

Some remnants survive from the Benedictine monastery, such as the particularly beautiful doorway, the *Porta Ferrada*, dating from the 11th c. The Arab influence is unmistakable. On the mountain ridge of Castellar stands the *Ermitage de Sant Elmo*, a hermitage which was dedicated in the 15th c. to the patron saint of seafarers and fishermen.

🏨 Tourism in Sant Feliu has developed extensively. So far, however, it still retains the character of a commercial town and port. Sant Feliu is certainly not a quiet place.

⛱ The main bathing beach lies in the harbour district. The neighbouring beaches and bays can be recommended, especially those on the road to S'Agaró, some of which are suitable for small children.

Rowing boats for hire.

 Children's playgrounds, round-abouts and bumper cars on the promenade.

 Casa Buxo (fish specialities, snails and mussels).

 Several cafés with dancing, and discothèques.

 Fiesta Mayor de Sant Feliu, from August 1st–4th.

 A pleasant change is a trip to the great wine cellars of Llagostera about 15 km inland (coach or car-hire).

From Sant Feliu to Tossa (23 km) runs one of the most beautiful coast roads in Europe. Above the steep and rugged cliffs it twists and turns through forests of cork-oaks and pine trees. The ever-changing view provides new and enchanting panoramas; the blue-green shimmer of the bays, large and small, the russet glow of the rocky slopes and cliffs — an interplay of colour and form of incredible beauty. About half-way between Sant Feliu and Tossa a minor road branches off to the *Hermitage of Sant Grau* (5 km), which is well worth a visit because from here you have the best all-round view over this truly 'wild' part of the Costa Brava.

Small and large holiday villages are springing up everywhere, with apart-ment blocks and bungalows, swimming pools, tennis courts and many other holiday amenities.

Tossa de Mar Pop. 2600

This is the biggest resort on the Costa Brava after Lloret. Once a quiet fishing village, it owes its rapid development during recent years to its favourable and at the same time romantic position on a gently sweeping and protected bay.

Remains of the 4th c. Roman settlement of Turissa have survived. Like many coastal settlements in the area, the village was strongly fortified in the Middle Ages against pirate attacks. This village, the *Vila Vella* (12th c.), is well preserved and is one of the most attractive sights on the Costa Brava. It clings to the slope of a protective hill which rises from a small peninsula jutting out into the sea, and is surrounded by a fortress wall with five small and three large towers. (Today a lighthouse stands in place of the fourth tower on top of the hill.) A beautiful road, the Camí de Ronda, leads past the lighthouse to the ruins of a Gothic church, with a magnificent view over the bay of Tossa and out as far as Lloret. On the way back you pass through the terraced and uncommonly picturesque little streets of Vila Vella, where the *Tossa Museum* is also to be found. Here can be seen an impressive collection of pictures of Tossa and its surroundings, including works by Marc Chagall and Juan Serra.

Tossa is a lively place, not suitable for visitors seeking peace and quiet.

 The beach is about 500 m long and of coarse sand. In the high season it can scarcely cope with the influx of visitors. A happy alternative is the smaller beach of *La Bauma* further north, or *Mar Menuda*. The most beautiful spots, of course, are the little concealed bays below the road to Sant Feliu, some of which are accessible only by water. For small children, however, none of these bathing places is really suitable.

 Rowing boats for hire.

 Riding stables with instructors and opportunities to go out riding.

 Maria Angela in Vila Vella.

 Some discothèques.

A drink under the palms at Lloret de Mar

 El Ruedo.

 Lovely walks through the cork and pine forests inland.

 Nobody should miss a trip along the coast road to Sant Feliu. You can make this a circular tour: go on the scheduled ship, the 'Cruceros Costa Brava', and return by bus. It takes at least half a day, but of course you can spend longer there if you wish.

Lloret de Mar Pop. 8200

12 km south-west of Tossa lies the biggest resort on the Costa Brava, if judged by its capacity to take visitors rather than the number of inhabitants. It has experienced rapid development in recent years, and this is still going on. Together with Tossa, Lloret has played the main role in making the Costa Brava internationally competitive in attracting the mass tourism of recent years.

Lloret was founded in Roman times. In the course of the 18th c. it became an important town for maritime trade. Many of its inhabitants emigrated to America, and in the twilight of their lives they returned home, quite prosperous, and did all they could to improve the appearance of the town. The impressive private houses, which are still to be seen today, were built by these rich returning emigrants.

The beach at Lloret de Mar

In the immediate vicinity, and well worth seeing, are the ruins of the *Castle of Sant Joan*, with a splendid view, as well as the Romanesque church of the *Sant Quirze Hermitage*, and — 5 km away — the little monastery of *La Mare de Deu de Gracia* which dates from the 11th c. and from which there is a fine view.

Lloret is an extremely lively place, which quite deliberately places more value on the entertainment needs of its visitors than on their needs for relaxation.

The 1-km-long beach of coarse sand is wide enough to provide space for everybody in the high season. It falls away rather steeply into the sea, and for that reason is not suitable for small children and non-swimmers. However, on both sides of the main beach there are a number of smaller bays. Motor boats of the *Viajes Marítimos*, which ply between Blanes and Tossa, also go regularly to the bigger bays of Platja de Canyelles (in the Tossa direction) and Platja de Fanals (towards Blanes).

On the road to Girona.

4 riding stables, 2 with instructors. Opportunities to go out riding.

Rowing boats for hire.

Water-skiing school.

International kindergarten, trampoline, bumper cars.

Skittles in the open air.

  Casino with restaurant.

 El Trull (luxury class).

Gran Placa international cabaret with flamenco dancing. Also the famous Flamenco Shows in *Relicario, La Masia* and *Cabra d'Or*.

Fiesta Mayor from July 24th -26th, with ship processions, sardana, the original dance *ses Moratxes* and a grand firework display.

Large choice of walks through the highlands of the hinterland.

10 minutes by bus to *Marineland* in Palafolls (see page 57).

Between Lloret and Blanes (5 km) it is worth stopping to walk through the tropical Botanical Garden of *Piña de Rosa*, which vies for beauty with the Blanes Botanical Garden. Do not fail to visit the former *Hermitage of Santa Cristina* above the Platja de Boadella, a magnificent bathing bay, easy to reach from the road, but also served by the vessels of the *Viajes Marítimos*. The hermitage has a café for visitors, in the garden of which you can relax in the welcome shade of the massive pine trees. This is where the traditional procession of the fishermen of Lloret ends, with a banquet under the biggest of the pines, the legendary *El Gros*.

Blanes Pop. 20,000

The old fishing town and port marks the point where the Costa Brava comes to an end — or indeed begins. Recently some industrial firms have settled here.

Blanes is presumed to be the Roman Blanda, which was even mentioned by the writer Pliny. More recently, the harbour and shipyards of Blanes again became important when free trade with America brought prosperity.

A unique sight on the Costa Brava is the *Botanical Garden*, the life's work of the German, Carlos Faust. Here can be

Lloret de Mar

Botanical Garden at Blanes

seen a complete collection of Mediterranean flora.

Worthy of note is the very beautiful doorway of the *Parish Church of Santa Maria*, dating from the 14th c. The *Gothic fountain* in the Carrer Ample is of about the same date.

 Like all ports, Blanes is a comparatively lively place.

The 1-km-long beach is of coarse sand and very spacious, but not very suitable for children and non-swimmers.

S Sailing schools.

 Diving school.

Rowing boats for hire.

U Riding stables, with instruction.

Children's playground.

Several discothèques.

La Parilla (fish specialities).

A lovely path along the coast to Cala de Sant Francesc. Rewarding walks to beautiful viewpoints in the hinterland (e.g. Castell de Sant Joan).

5 minutes by bus to Palafolls' *Marineland* (see page 57).

The Hinterland

Girona

The airport is the only part of Girona that a lot of Costa Brava holidaymakers actually see. That is a pity, because the old terraced town on the three rivers of Ter, Güell and Onyar is well worth a visit. It lies only some 40 km inland, and is not more than an hour's journey by car from most places on the coast. The bus services are good too and travel agencies in the resorts arrange plenty of excursions. As the old town, which is the more interesting part, is concentrated into a small area, it only takes up half a day, and you will not have to walk for miles seeking out the sights.

 History

Girona, the provincial capital 'responsible' for the Costa Brava, has a very long history. Its origin goes right back to the Iberians; the Romans named it Gerunda, the Moors Dscherunda. After the expulsion of the Mussulmans (Muslims), who created havoc here, Girona fell to the counts of Barcelona and subsequently shared in the fortunes

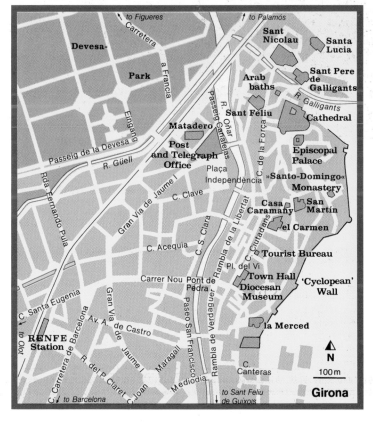

Girona

Girona old town

of Catalan and, later, Aragonese-Catalan history (see page 12). The kings of Aragón were also called 'Princes of Girona'.

In the 13th c. the kings of France would have liked to annex Girona which was strategically important to them. However, in 1285 Philip the Bold had to call off the siege of the town, because the fighting strength of his army suffered under the onslaught of vast swarms of flies and gnats. Since then the people of Girona have sung the praises of the 'Mochas de Sant Narcis', the Flies of Saint Narcissus, for it is said that they came from the coffin containing his bones. However, it appears that the flies no longer attack tourists today.

The centuries which followed were a period of peace and prosperity for Girona; this is clearly indicated by the buildings of the old town. Not until the 17th c. did the freshly awakened covetousness of the French bring further war and occupation to the country. The boundary formed by the Pyrenees was then by no means as natural as it appears to us today. The Gironese added a glorious page to the history of their town, however, when in 1809, during the Napoleonic Wars, a small Spanish force held out for seven months against a superior French besieging army.

Sightseeing

The visitor has sight of his first and most impressive view of historic Girona from the Onyar bridges, which link the new parts of the town with the self-contained heart of the old town. From the Carrer Nou you pass over the Pont de Pedra to the *Plaça del Vi*. Surrounded by shady arcades, it invites you to sit, drink and watch the world go by, while the more serious art buffs will perhaps prefer to visit the *Diocesan Museum* with its display of ecclesiastical art from past centuries. (The museum is open daily, but only from 11 a.m. to 1 p.m.) A noteworthy and attractive building in the square is the 15th c. *Ajuntament* (town hall).

On the way to the cathedral you pass state-owned mansion houses and go through the Carrer Ciutadans, Carrer de Zapaterijas Viejas and Carrer de la Força. This brings you to the foot of the great flight of 86 steps leading up to the *cathedral*. The tower dating from 1580 and the 18th c. façade give no indication of the fact that the Gothic interior of the church is based on one of the boldest technical designs of the time. The plan of the architect Bofill in 1417 was that Girona should build a church with a single nave with the greatest span of any in the world — and build it they did, 23 m wide, 35 m high and 63 m long. The mere figures are not in themselves particularly exciting, but this church which, despite its great size, appears almost plain is in fact an overwhelming experience. There are beautiful windows in the apse, and in the choir is an elaborate 11th c. alabaster altar which was taken from the old church.

On the left of the entrance is the triple

Arch of the 'Palau d'Agullana', Girona

chapter-house, in which the church treasure is kept. Here the admiration of connoisseurs is inspired by the great 11th c. tapestry depicting in detail the story of the Creation. Amongst the many other treasures the Romanesque wooden sculpture of the Virgin Mary (12th c.) is particularly beautiful. That is not all: near the chapter-house you will find one of the most splendid cloisters in all of Spain, dating from the 12th and 13th c. and in a mixture of Romanesque and Gothic styles. The capitals of the columns are richly decorated with ornaments and figures. You could spend hours studying the Old and New Testament stories which they depict.

You now descend the steps again, turn right and come to the church of *Sant Feliu*, the Gothic bell tower of which is one of the most characteristic features of the town. The church is built on the spot where, in early Christian times, Saint Felix and Saint Narcissus (the aforementioned saint of the flies) were said to have suffered a martyr's death. The major part of it was built in the 14th c. but the façade dates from the 17th c. Inside the church can be seen eight Roman and early Christian sarcophagi which are artistically among the most important of their period.

Not far from the church of Sant Feliu are the *Arab Baths* (Banys àrabs), which date not from the Arab period but from the 12th or 13th c. So lasting was the Moorish influence, however, that some hundreds of years later these baths still reflected the Arab love of bathing.

Crossing the mainly dry river-bed of the Riu Galligants you arrive in front of the Romanesque church of *Sant Pere de Galligants* where you can wander through a magnificent cloister with beautiful 12th c. capitals on the columns.

It is well worth while taking a walk through the Passeig Arqueològic and down through one of the narrow little streets, with their delightful inner courtyards and old façades, to arrive at the *Call Judío* quarter to the right of the Carrer de la Força; Call Judío was where the Jews of Gerunda lived from the 9th to the end of the 15th century.

La Bisbal d'Empordà Pop. 7500

Depending on where you start out from, an excursion to Girona can be combined with a trip to La Bisbal d'Empordà and the surrounding area. La Bisbal d'Empordà itself is an interesting provincial town. This is the home of the potter's art. In the potteries along the main road from La Bisbal to Girona you will find a wide choice of old and new glazed tiles and decorative and practical ceramics.

Monells (some 7 km north-west of La Bisbal) is a small medieval village with a particularly impressive market place.

Ullastret (about 5 km north-east of La Bisbal) offers excavations of an Iberian settlement, of little interest to the layman. The archaeological finds are on display in the *Museu Monografic del Poblat Ibèric*.

Peratallada (about 4 km north-east of La Bisbal) is a very well preserved medieval village of Empordà. It is at its most beautiful at sunset. Some charming Catalan restaurants invite you to partake of a typical evening meal. The *Castell* of Peratallada, which was until 1985 in the private possession of the Condes (counts) of Torroella, is open to visitors. In July and August concerts are held in the castle armoury.

Pals (some 11 km east of La Bisbal) is surrounded by old walls. There is the Gothic church of *Sant Pere* to be seen, together with the massive Romanesque tower, *Torre de las Hores*, and typical, prettily restored and well tended houses. From the *Torre de Roma* there is a magnificent view over the countryside.

Costa Daurada: the Maresme

Names and terms can be rather confusing. You may have read in an older holiday guide that it is the Costa Levantina which adjoins the Costa Brava, yet now it is called the Costa Daurada and the Maresme. It is, however, one and the same strip of coast; it is simply that one name has been replaced by another which was felt to be more attractive and more effective from a publicity point of view.

For Costa Daurada means 'Coast of Gold'. That does not mean that you can hope to pan successfully for gold here, it just refers to the colour of the sand, and in that respect those who created the name of the coast of gold were not exaggerating.

Maresme, however, is the name of the countryside between the Costa Brava and Barcelona, bordered by the rivers Tordera in the north and Besòs in the south. This stretch of land, blessed with a fine climate and fertile soil, is famous for its cultivation of fruit, vegetables, lettuce and flowers; among the latter, carnations enjoy a special status. They are produced on an industrial basis, and are an important export item and earner of foreign currency. The fields of carnations display the full magic of their blaze of colour at a time of year when few tourists can enjoy it; in February and March — when early spring bulbs are beginning to flower in Britain — a fragrant and multi-tinted veil of blooms covers the fields.

Malgrat Pop. 10,500

This is an unimpressive industrial town, which also has an iron mine. Even though it possesses 5 km of beach of coarse sand, with plenty of room for bathing, it really cannot be recommended as a place to stay on holiday.

Quite near, however, 5 km inland in Palafolls, *Marineland* has become an attraction for young and old. It was the first Marine Park in Spain, offering performances with dolphins, sea-lions and parrots, as well as a show by pearl divers. The park is a real holiday

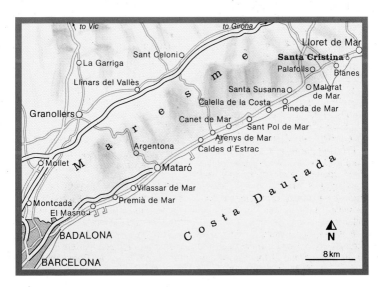

treat for children and a welcome change from the beach.

Santa Susanna Pop. 500

This is an up-and-coming resort, although as yet there are no tourist facilities apart from hotels and holiday flats. The level beach is very good for children. However, Santa Susanna — like many of the places about to be described — suffers from the fact that the railway line and part of the main highway separate the town from the beach.

Pineda de Mar Pop. 10,600

Pineda de Mar is developing into an impressive resort. It has 2 km of beach with coarse sand, and is a quiet place particularly suitable for families with children.

🔱 Riding stables.

⛵ Rowing boats for hire.

🛝 Children's playground. 🎿 ⛺

Calella de la Costa Pop. 10,000

Not to be confused with the scenically more attractive but smaller and less well known Calella de Palafrugell, Calella de la Costa is a favourite with the Germans, and has thus acquired the nickname 'Calella de los Alemanes'. The former fishing village has changed over almost completely to the tourist trade.

🏨 Visitors seeking peace and quiet will not get their money's worth here. Calella is only for those wanting lively entertainment.

🏖 2 km of coarse sand.

⛵ Rowing boats for hire.

🔱 Including night rides with bivouac.

🛝 Children's playground in a small park; fairground (with bumper cars etc.) on the beach.

🍴 *La Olla* (Spanish specialities); *Casa Carreras* (Catalan specialities; rather out of the way).

🎵 Lots of discothèques.

🍷 *Las Cuevas* night club.

✂ Fiesta Mayor June 16th–17th; Sept. 23rd–25th.

💃 Catalan *Sardana Festival* on the first Sunday in June.

🚶 Pretty walks in the hilly hinterland.

🚌 Excursions by horse-drawn carriages can be arranged.

Sant Pol de Mar Pop. 2000

This is a resort with various strips of beach with coarse and fine sand. Railway line and main road run through the town, the houses of which are grouped around a 10th/11th c. monastery.

Canet de Mar Pop. 7500

Canet is not only an important industrial town (cork industry; well known for lace-making), but it is also developing into a popular resort. Worth seeing are the *medieval castle* and the *Castell Santa Florentina*.

🏨 A quiet place, apart from the road and rail traffic.

🏖 A lovely, spacious beach with fine sand.

🚶 Pretty walks in the hilly hinterland, with splendid viewing points.

⛵ Rowing boats for hire.

🔱 Riding stables with opportunities to go out riding.

Santa Susanna

Calella de la Costa

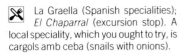 La Graella (Spanish specialities); *El Chaparral* (excursion stop). A local speciality, which you ought to try, is cargols amb ceba (snails with onions).

 4 discothèques.

Arenys de Mar Pop. 10,000
Arenys is important as a fishing, commercial and, above all, yachting port. Bathing comes second.

Arenys stands on ancient Roman foundations. It had a good reputation as a port as long ago as the Middle Ages.

The following are worth seeing:

The *Torre dels Encantats* is an imposing fortress built over a pre-Roman settlement in the 13th/14th c. The parish church has one of the most beautiful Baroque altars in Catalonia (dated 1706). Interesting archaeological finds and ceramics are shown in the museum. Every Saturday a big market is held in Arenys which is worth visiting.

As a harbour town, Arenys is busy with a lot of traffic — main road and railway line run through it — and offers little in the way of peace and quiet.

The beach of fine sand is relatively small, and not really suitable for children and non-swimmers.

Rowing boats for hire.

 Water-skiing school.

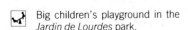

Big children's playground in the *Jardin de Lourdes* park.

Posito (fish specialities); *Portinyol* (Catalan specialities, a little way out of town).

Fiesta Mayor from July 8th-11th and from August 15th-16th.

Lovely walks along the coast, for example to Canet and in the mountainous hinterland in the wooded valley of Vallagorguina.

Caldes d'Estrac (Caldetes)
Pop. 1200
Seaside resort and spa, rich in tradition, with a beautiful beach promenade.

The beach is broken up into a number of little bays and is of rather coarse sand. Not really suitable for small children.

Rowing boats for hire.

H Thermal Baths (41°C).

From Caldes to Barcelona
It is only about a further 40 km from Caldes d'Estrac to Barcelona. Along the coast, closer and closer together, you will find places such as Mataró, Vilassar de Mar, Premià de Mar and El Masnou. Although they describe themselves as resorts, and are so to a degree, they are not recommended for a regular stay on holiday. While they do have some nice sections of beach, the proximity of Barcelona is made only too obvious by a lot of industrialisation and — when winds are in the wrong quarter — by water which is far from clean.

The last town before Barcelona is Badalona, population 90,000, a purely industrial town which will soon merge into the metropolis. It is best to take the motorway in Mataró to Barcelona, as this runs along the mountain slopes and offers lovely views of the coast.

Barcelona

Your initial impression of Barcelona may well be that it is a somewhat featureless place, similar to many other large cities. However, although Barcelona can scarcely be called beautiful it is certainly fascinating, and the more you get to know it the more interesting it becomes. As you will probably not have the time to explore the city thoroughly, some of the principal points of interest are highlighted below.

First of all, a few details: Barcelona lies on a 4–6-km-wide coastal plain, between the sea and a semicircle of small mountains, to which it owes its delightful situation and sheltered climate. With its 3 million inhabitants, it is the largest city in Spain after Madrid and an important industrial centre (textiles, chemicals, ironworks and ship-building). Many big and small commercial firms also have their headquarters here. The rapid economic development of the city can be seen from the fact that in 1940 it had only 1.1 million inhabitants. However, Barcelona has lost much of its former importance as a port, and it is now largely bypassed by international shipping.

Barcelona, the historical metropolis of the Catalans and the capital city of the province of the same name, is today also the seat of provincial government, of parliament

Strolling in the Ramblas

View over Barcelona

and of the archbishop.

It possesses the largest opera house in Spain (the *Liceu*), a thriving artistic life, an influential press, two bullrings and, in FC Barcelona, one of the most famous football clubs in Europe.

In brief, Barcelona is a centre for the most varied activities, and one of the liveliest cities in Europe.

 ## A Glimpse of the past

Barcelona is assumed to have been founded by the Greek Phocaeans from Massilia (Marseilles) or Emporion (Empúries, see page 34). The Carthaginians settled here for a time, the Romans for much longer. In A.D. 514 it was conquered by the Visigoths and became their capital for a period. Between 713 and 801 it was in the hands of the Arabs, and when they were driven out the Franks made it the capital of their border area. After the counts of Barcelona had made themselves independent, it became the capital of the powerful and ambitious kingdom of Catalonia until it was

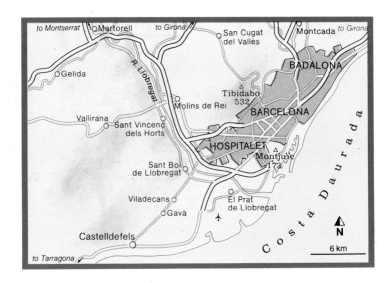

united through marriage with that of Aragón.

What the city thereby lost in political power it gained in international standing and economic importance. The Maritime Law, which was drawn up in Barcelona in 1258, became internationally enforceable. Next to Venice and Genoa, Catalonia-Barcelona became the dominant maritime power in the Mediterranean. Trade prospered under the protection of the fleet; the city became one of the most important banking centres in Europe. From this period date the most representative monuments of old Barcelona.

When, in the year 1474, following the marriage of Ferdinand of Aragón to Isabella of Castile, Catalonia became a province of the newly formed national state of Spain, Barcelona was relegated to a provincial city. After the discovery of America Spain turned entirely towards the Atlantic; that meant a further decline in influence and prosperity because the Catalans were not allowed to trade with America.

The centuries which followed were not very happy ones for Barcelona. As the Catalans, confidently struggling for independence, revolted time and again against the central state governing from Madrid, they always found themselves 'on the wrong side': in the Spanish War of Succession, during the Carlist uprisings and other internal conflicts in the 19th c., and ultimately in the Civil War of 1936–39. Yet their unshakeable vitality and dynamism always brought them back on to their feet again. During the last hundred years Barcelona has expanded in economic strength, in population and in other unprecedented ways, as witnessed by the extensive new development outside the boundary of the old city. The Spanish Civil War, during which Barcelona was a republican stronghold and remained in their hands until the end, left deep scars. Nevertheless, the city's vitality became even stronger, and today it is not only the most progressive but also the most prosperous city in Spain.

A Day in Barcelona

To begin with — some tips on how to allocate your time. Anyone who holidays on the Costa Brava or on the Costa Daurada normally plans a trip to Barcelona. He sets off after breakfast, arrives in Barcelona — depending on his starting point — between 10 and 11 a.m., and leaves again at 6 p.m. at the latest, so as to be back at the hotel in time for dinner. This way of splitting up the day is the worst possible, for it means that you make your planned visits during the hot and tiring midday and afternoon (and you cannot see everything you would like because most of the museums and other buildings are closed anyway) and then leave the city when it is at its best, namely when it comes to life in the evening. So if you cannot manage to stay overnight, which is definitely the best solution, why not vary the normal course of events and travel to Barcelona at midday, seek the cool of the churches and museums from about 3 p.m. onwards and then join in the life of the city in the evening. Travel back at midnight — why not? You are on holiday and can rest the next day . . .

'Share in the life of the city' — that is an important maxim. Barcelona is much richer in art treasures and things to see than is generally assumed. That is why you should not try to keep to a strict programme of places to visit; it is not possible within one or two days. Just go as you please, wander through the streets, study the people, visit a bar or café, do just what takes your fancy — in that way you will get a lot more out of Barcelona. This is the way you should read our 'circular tour': do not follow it blindly, but vary it and go where and when you want — it's always the best way!

A stroll through the city

The Ramblas Our starting point is the *Plaça de Catalunya* (see page 66), the link, so to speak, between the old city

Plaça de Cataluna Escultura de Clara

and the new districts, and a particularly splendid and spacious square. This is where the famous *Ramblas* begin, which, 1200 m in length, cut through the old town and form the main artery of the life of the city. Although they are open to traffic they are predominantly a series of pedestrian promenades, with shady canopies of plane trees, and shops, restaurants, cafés, theatres and cinemas to left and to right, a flower market, bird market, rows of seats — you can walk up and down three or four times and still see the scene in a different light and with a different cast. You really must go into the *Mercat de Josep* (La Boquería), the great market hall on the right-hand side, and gaze at the sheer quantity and variety of fish and other seafood all laid out so appetisingly! A contrast, so typical of Barcelona, is the famous Opera House nearby (*Gran Teatre del Liceu*) with its 5000 seats.

Barri Gòtic Broadly speaking the Ramblas divide the old town into the *Barri Xino* on the right-hand side (we will come back to that later) and the *Barri Gòtic* (Gothic quarter) on the left, which you enter along the Carrer Ferran. You then come to the Plaça de Sant Jaume, where you will find the *Ajuntament* (city

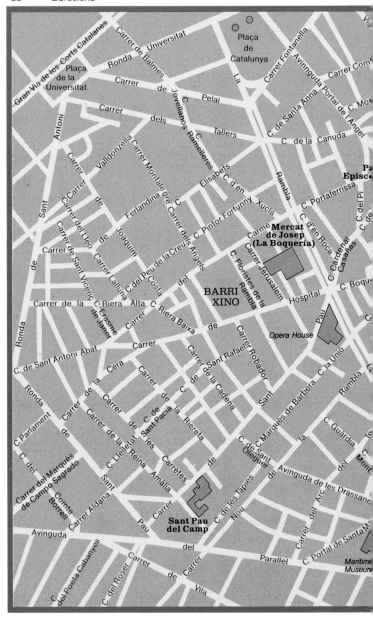

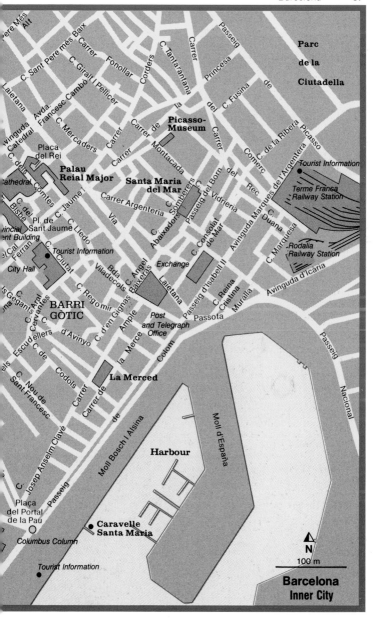

Parc
de la
Ciutadella

C. Pere Mès Alt

C. Sant Pere mès Baix

Carrer Fonollar

C. Giralt I Pellicer

C. Sant Pere mès Baix

Laietana

Avda.
Francesc Cambó

C. Mercaders

Avinguda
Catedral

Plaça
del Rei

**Palau
Reial Major**

Cathedral

C. dels Comtes

C. del Bisbe

C. Jaume I

Pl. de
Sant Jaume

C. Lledó

Via

C. Ferran

Provincial
Government Building

del Call

City Hall

Tourist Information

C. Ciutat

Carrer Princesa

C. Tantarantana

Corders

Carrer de

Carrer de

Carrer Montacada

**Picasso-
Museum**

Carrer Princesa

C. Fusina

de la

Carrer

**Santa Maria
del Mar**

Carrer Argenteria

Carrer del

Passeig

C. de la Ribera

Picasso

Tourist Information

**Terme Franša
Railway Station**

Avinguda Marques de l'Argentera

C. Duana

C. Sombrerers

Passeig del Born

C. Vidrieria

Comerç

del

Rec

C. Consolat de Mar

C. Abaixadors

Exchange

Passeig d'Isabell II

Laietana

C. Reina
Cristina

Muralla

C. Marquesa

**Rodalia
Railway Station**

Avinguda d'Icària

BARRI
GÒTIC

C. Aral

C. Cervantes

C. Escudellers

d'Avinyo

C. d'en Gignas

Bda. Viladecols

C. Angel
Baixeras

C. Regomir

Ample

C. Nou de
Sant Francesc

Codols

Carrer de

de

la Merce

Colom

Post
and Telegraph
Office

Passota

C. de

La Merced

Josep Anselm Clave

Passeig

Plaça
del Portal
de la Pau

Columbus Column

**Caravelle
Santa Maria**

Tourist Information

Moll Bosch i Alsina

Harbour

Moll d'Espanya

Passeig

Nacional

N

100 m

**Barcelona
Inner City**

Above and below: In the Barri Gòtic (Gothic Quarter)

hall) with its beautiful Gothic inner courtyard; opposite is the seat of the provincial government, a pure late Gothic building apart from the façade.

Passing through the Carrer Bisbe you come to the *cathedral*, and then to its magnificent Gothic cloisters with a pond containing geese and goldfish. The cathedral itself is considered to be one of the most important Gothic buildings in Spain. It was built between 1398 and 1448 on the site of a former Romanesque church at the highest point in old Barcelona. The façade dates from the 19th c. and the dome from the year 1913. The triple-aisled interior, with its slender fluted columns rising in a subdued and mysterious light, is impressively elegant. Two things stand out among the rich fittings of the interior: in the crypt is a superb marble sarcophagus of the Italian school (1327) for the remains of Saint Eulalia, and in the first chapel to the right of the main doorway, can be seen a black crucifix which John of Austria is said to have had with him at the naval battle of Lepanto, and which helped him to victory. Finally, there are the finely carved choir stalls, showing the names and coats of arms of the knights whom Charles V admitted into the Order of Saint Vlies.

Close to the cathedral lies the charming Plaça del Rei with the *Palau Reial Major*, in which at one time the counts of Barcelona and later of Aragón resided. The jewel of the palace is the Sala Tinell, a Romanesque function room with a wide-spanned vaulted roof. This is where Ferdinand of Aragón and Isabella of Castile, their 'Catholic Majesties', received Christopher Columbus on his return from America. The Sala Tinell, together with the Municipal History Museum, is open to visitors from 11 a.m. to 2 p.m. and from 4 to 8 p.m.

The Gothic quarter has a wealth of historical treasures, including numerous remains of walls from Roman times. We can select only a few, but anyone who keeps his eyes open as he wanders through the colourful maze of old streets and alleyways will spot something worth seeing at every step, will make his own discoveries and find pleasure in the fact that the bustling activity means there is nothing museum-like about this quarter.

Anyone keen on investigating Catalan Gothic still further should go from the Via Laietana to the Carrer de Montcada. Here you can admire former palaces in Gothic and Baroque architecture which today house the city's best-known art galleries. The *Picasso Museum* has an international reputation. Then you come to the church of *Santa Maria del Mar*, a triple-naved church dating from the 14th c. with a very beautiful doorway, and continuing towards the harbour you find the *Llotja* (Stock Exchange), with its imposing late Gothic interior (1392).

As we have said, the harbour is not particularly exciting, and you can dispense with making a trip round it. More interesting is the *Maritime Museum* at the Plaça del Portal de la Pau; it is housed in a shipyard, the oldest parts of which date from the 14th c. — something you will not find anywhere else in Europe. In the middle of the square stands the 60-m-high *Columbus Monument*, from the upper gallery of which (lift) there is a fine view over the city and the harbour. Also dedicated to the memory of Columbus is a faithful reproduction of his ship, the 'Santa Maria', which lies in the harbour and is open to visitors. A cableway crosses the harbour, ending at Montjuïc. On the opposite side of the harbour you can see Barceloneta, founded in 1755 as the suburb of the fishermen and port workers, with numerous picturesque lanes.

The Plaça del Portal de la Pau forms the end of the Ramblas, along which you should return as far as the Plaça Reial, where you turned off into the Barri Gòtic.

Barri Xino The popular amusement quarter of Barcelona, begins here on the

Above: C. Bisbe Irurita.
Below: Columbus Monument

Pueblo Español

left side of the Ramblas. It does not really come to life until the late evening. It differs little from the sleazy districts of other ports.

In this it is assumed that you have only one day at your disposal. However, that is nowhere near long enough to see all that is worth seeing in Barcelona. If you can stay longer, there are some suggestions that we would like to make.

Montjuïc A hill about 200 m high in the south of the town, above the harbour. It is best to take a taxi. On the hill is a *Military Museum* with an interesting collection of weapons. There is also a grand view over the town and harbour from here. You return to the city along pleasant roads through pretty surroundings. Everything is at its best in the early mornings. If you are an art-lover you should find time to visit the *Fundació Miró*. On Montjuïc is the *Pueblo Espanol* (Spanish Village), which was erected in 1929 at the time of the International Exhibition, with houses reproduced true to the style of the various Spanish regions, as well as some typical Spanish arts and crafts. Near the village stands the *Museu d' Arte de Catalunya* (Museum of Catalan Art), open from 9 a.m. to 1 p.m., except Monday. It has a unique collection of

Montjuïc

Romanesque paintings and sculpture, mainly from Spanish towns in the Pyrenees. Close by is the *Museu Arqueològic* (Archaeological Museum), open from 10 a.m. to 6 p.m., with a rich collection of Spanish pre-history, including excavation finds from Emporion-Empúries. Both are amongst the top-ranking European museums.

Sagrada Familia The four strange 100-m-tall towers of this church are visible from almost everywhere. Intensive work is being carried out on what should be a giant building (the dome alone will be 160 m high). How the final construction will look can be seen from the model displayed in what will be part of the crypt. There is a wonderful view over the city from the towers. The unconventional architect, Antoni Gaudí (1852–1926), who intended that the church should be a 'sermon in stone' and 'the cathedral of all cathedrals', is recognised worldwide. It is said of Gaudí that 'he has impressed the stamp of his genius on modern Barcelona'. Everywhere you go you meet the strangely bizarre work of this architect. One of his typical works is the *Palau Güell* (1885) in the Nou de la Rambla, a side street off the Ramblas, and two more houses can be seen in the

Monument to the Sardana, Montjuïc

main shopping street, Passeig de Gràcia; the distinctive design and the equally distinctive use of materials make the two houses of *Batlló* and *Milá* stand out among the thousands of others of the same period.

A delightful walk can be taken through the *Parc Güell*, in the upper part of the city.

Tibidabo A 532-m-high hill north-west of the city, with a magnificent view not only over the city and the sea, but also over the countryside inland. It can be reached by public transport (underground railway, tram and cable car or rack railway), but we would recommend

a taxi (it takes about 1/2 hour from the Ramblas). That way you will not only save time but also enjoy the trip along the beautiful main street with lots to see. The buildings on the hill are less pleasing. As well as a number of restaurants there are a water tower, a large modern church (*Sagrado Corazón*, 1935) with an oversized statue of Christ, and a fairground. You can take a pretty walk along the crest of the hill to the villas in Vallvidrera with its lovely old parish church.

 Spanish Catalan

In Barcelona you can try out the whole

Sagrada Familia

Sagrado Corazón, Tibidabo

culinary range. However, we suggest omitting the luxury restaurants and concentrating on Spanish-Catalan cooking. Typical restaurants serving good plain fare are, for example, *Los Caracoles*, 14 Carrer Escudellers (side street off the Ramblas); *Sieta Puertas*, 14 Passeig d'Isabel II (near the Stock Exchange); *Carballeira*, 3 Carrer Reina Cristina (near the Stock Exchange).

In the port — between the Ramblas and Via Laietana — as well as in the fishing suburb of Barceloneta, there are numerous quite modest inns, known as *merenderos*, where you can get excellent fish and shellfish fresh from the sea.

Finally there are the tapas, the virtues of which we have already extolled. They are not only cheap but also have the advantage that you can enjoy them going along, without losing too much time. One of the most productive sources of tapas in Barcelona is the Plaça Reial with its many cafés.

 Montserrat Monastery

Barcelona is also the starting point for a visit to Montserrat ('hewn out of a hill') and its famous monastery (about 50 km north-west; daily buses from the Plaça de la Universitat). The bizarre rock

Tibidabo

massif — a conglomerate of stone deposits which originated on the sea-bed and were forced up over the course of many centuries — has a grandiose appearance. For the local people it is a symbol of its faith and the goal of the many pilgrims who come to pay homage to the Black Madonna, the patron saint of Catalonia. At 12 noon the boys' choir (l'Escolania) sings the 'Salve'. The monastery owns some priceless treasures, including its famous library of 200,000 volumes. When visibility is good it is worth while taking the cable-car to Sant Jeroni peak (1236 m), from where there are interesting walks with splendid views over the countryside.

Modern Barcelona
One of many excellent restaurants in Barcelona

Montserrat Monastery
Casa Milá, Barcelona

Costa Daurada: south of Barcelona

The coastline between Barcelona and Tarragona is by no means as straight as it is depicted on some maps. Admittedly, neither to the north-east nor to the south-west of Barcelona can the Costa Daurada offer such rugged and inaccessible parts as the Costa Brava does in its 'wildest' places, but the eye is never bored by the apparently endless strip of coast. Rocky spits of land form numerous bays, big and small, and these alternate with gently curving gulfs. Constancy in change — that could be the theme of this distinctive coastal landscape. The tightly winding cliff road between Castelldefels and Sitges is a match, as regards natural beauty, for the more famous road between Sant Feliu de Guíxols and Tossa. In the fertile hinterland, amongst Roman relics, ruined castles and monasteries, are grown the grapes from which Penedès wine is made. This has been enthusiastically consumed by all who have passed this way: Iberians and Celts, Carthaginians and Romans, Goths and Normans — and 20th c. tourists.

You will find it interesting to visit the champagne cellars of Sant Sadurní d'Anoia, about 20 km west of Barcelona, on the motorway to Tarragona.

Sitges

Castelldefels Pop. 20,000

A lively resort which, being so near to Barcelona, is popular for weekend outings. It was mentioned in the Middle Ages as the 'Castello de los fieles' (Castle of the Faithful), a tribute to its loyalty to the king of Aragón.

You should visit the ruins of the castle which dates from the 14th and 15th c. The Romanesque church houses a beautiful Madonna dating from Carolingian times.

 4 km of sandy beach, suitable for children.

  Several discothèques.

 Fiesta Mayor August 15th/16th.

Sitges Pop. 14,000

Sitges is the most visited resort between Barcelona and Tarragona and one of the most elegant and original places on the Catalan coast. Particularly noteworthy is the magnificent long avenue of palm trees by the sea. On the Barcelona side of the town has grown up the *Aigua Dolç* yachting harbour; it is well worth taking a stroll through here and lingering a while, both during the day and in the evening, in the friendly cafés and bars. There is a true harbour atmosphere.

Sitges is mentioned in Roman times, but for many centuries was just an unimportant fishing village.

The little town has two interesting museums: the *Museu del Cau Ferrat* with works by El Greco, Rusíñol, Picasso and Utrillo amongst others, and the *Maricel Museum* with a good collection of paintings, drawings, ceramics, etc. The parish church on the hill dates from the 18th c.

While it is comparatively quiet in the residential quarter, there is a lot going on in the town and on the beach. Sitges is also known as the Spanish St Tropez!

Golf course (12 holes).

2-km-long, flat beach of fine sand.

Rowing boats for hire.

Children's playground, baby-sitting.

La Masía.

 Several discothèques and night clubs.

The new casino should be one of the best in Europe.

Famous Corpus Christi procession; procession of ships on July 16th; Fiesta Mayor from August 23rd-26th; horse and cycle racing.

Vilanova i la Geltrú Pop. 41,500

This is a modern industrial town with a picturesque fishing quarter and 3 km of fine sand stretching along both sides of the harbour. It has, however, little to recommend it as a long-stay resort.
Worth seeing is the *Castell de là Geltrú*, a massive castle with a square courtyard, dating in its present form from the 12th–14th c. In the castle is the *Museum of Balaguer* with an interesting collection of paintings, sculptures and a library of 40,000 volumes.

Several small fish restaurants along the harbour, providing good value for money.

Passing the little town of Cubellas, we leave Barcelona province and enter that of Tarragona. The resorts which follow offer the advantage of wide, flat beaches of fine sand, giving the bather more freedom of movement and 'room to breathe' than on most beaches in the better known resorts. *Segur de Calafell, Calafell, Sant Salvador* and *Comaruga* offer every imaginable kind of entertainment and sporting facilities.

Roda de Berà Pop. 1050

This township includes the urban area of Roc de Sant Gaietà, in which houses in the styles of various Spanish regions have been built. Worth the trip!

Torredembarra Pop. 3000

The resort has particularly clear, blue-green water and an offshore reef which is attractive to underwater swimmers.

It is a further 12 km from Torredembarra to Tarragona. On the way you pass Altafona and Tamarit, near the mouth of the river Gaià, above which towers a massive castle dating from the 12th to the 14th c. From the castle there is a beautiful view over the wide soft beaches of this part of the country.

Shortly before you reach Tarragona the Roman town announces its presence by means of some 'advance' monuments: a stone quarry, 200 m off the road to the right, which provided the materials for building the Roman town; a 2nd c. triumphal arch, *El Arc de Berà*, decorated in relief and standing in the middle of the road; and the *Torre dels Escipions* (Tower of the Scipios), also 2nd c., a mausoleum containing the bones of fallen Roman legionaries.

Tarragona Pop. 140,000

Unless you are completely insensitive to the aura of a thousand years of history, you should on no account fail to visit Tarragona. You will notice straight away that Tarragona is a friendly and

Tarragona Cathedral

agreeable town, and beautifully situated. Starting from the edge of an extensive bay, it climbs terrace-fashion up the side of a hill crowned by the great cathedral, providing a succession of enchanting views over the Mediterranean as far as the Ebro delta. The loveliest view of all is from the famous *Balcó del Mediterrani*, the impressive area at the end of the Rambla Nova, which is both the main artery and heart of the town.

Tarragona has about 140,000 inhabitants. It is the provincial capital, diocesan seat and an industrial town and port; in all, what one could term a varied and lively centre of some importance. Yet all this is but a pale reflection of its great past, for its historical zenith was reached some two thousand years ago.

The town's beginnings are lost in the impenetrable mists of the 3rd millennium B.C. It has been proved that the hill was already inhabited at that time. It is assumed that settlers came from the Aegean. In any event, the Iberians, who were 'at home' in the country, founded their town of Cesse there. The Greeks, too, had a trading base here — as they had in Emporion. The name they gave it says everything: *Kallipolis* or Beautiful Town!

During the Second Punic War, around the year 200 B.C., the Romans under the Scipios drove their mortal enemies, the Carthaginians, out of the town, named it Tarraco and made it their base for the conquest of Spain. Roman patricians and emperors, including Caesar, Augustus, Hadrian and others, visited it for relaxation or as a temporary residence. After the complete subjugation of the Iberian Peninsula, Tarraco became the capital of the Roman province of Hispania Citerior and, it is said, the second city after Rome itself. In its heyday, it is said to have had a million inhabitants and a city wall measuring 68 kilometres. In any event it possessed everything a great Roman city had to have — a temple, palaces, theatre and amphitheatre, a circus and a forum.

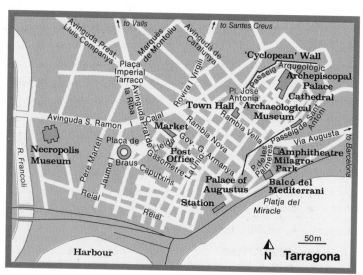

Parque Acüatico, Tarragona

The Christianisation of Spain also began in Tarraco. It is said to have been the Apostle Paul himself who converted the city. It later became the seat of the Spanish primate.

The decline of Tarraco-Tarragona began with the fall of the Roman Empire. It was of no importance under the Visigoths, and the Moors destroyed a large part of it in the year 714. The town's rulers changed frequently during the following centuries. Not until 1220 did Tarragona finally become Catalan.

 A tour of the Old Town

The starting point is the Balcó del Mediterrani, which has been mentioned before, and which continues on the left in the Passeig de les Palmeres. Below this viewing terrace can be seen the ruins of the *Amphitheatre*, built in the time of the Emperor Augustus. Historical monuments lie one on the other, like rock strata: on top of the Roman ruins can still be seen the remains of the walls of a Visigoth church and a Romanesque one. A flight of steps leads down to the Passeig de Sant Antoni. On the left is the *Augustus Palace*, which forms the western boundary of the former forum — further remains of which can be seen in the Plaça del Rei. The palace is also

Above: Amphitheatre. Below: Torre dels Escipions, Tarragona

known as Pretori Romà or Torréon Pilato, because it is said that Pilate, the famous 'Governor of Syria', once held the office of praetor (magistrate) here. Next to it stands the *Provincial Archaeological Museum*, with an extensive collection of finds from the Roman period: sarcophagi, sculptures, mosaics, coins and everyday articles, etc. (Open daily except Monday.)

From the Plaça del Rei you walk through the streets of the old town and up to the *cathedral*, built in the 12th and 13th c. on the highest point of the town, on the site of a former temple to Jupiter. Most impressive are the façade with the huge Gothic arched doorway, the figures flanking it (apostles and prophets) and the large rose window above.

In the interior, changes in contemporary tastes during the period it took to build can be clearly detected. The apse is still pure Romanesque and, because there was still a fear that the Moors might return, has a fortress-like character. The long nave and choir are early Gothic (13th c.) while the open side chapels display late Gothic or typically Spanish-Baroque styles (known in technical parlance as 'Plateresque' and 'Churrigueresque'). Some parts were not completed until the late 18th c.

Among the many beautiful works to be seen in the cathedral, the late Gothic choir stalls, the winged altar of St Michael (1432) in the chapel of the same name, and the superb upper part (1430) of the high altar deserve your special attention; the last named is a true miracle of the sculptor's art — carved from pure alabaster.

You leave the cathedral through the beautiful Romanesque east door (the carving on the tympanum depicting Christ enthroned with the symbols of the Evangelists) and enter the almost square cloister which, like the church itself, combines Romanesque and Gothic styles. It is also one of the most beautiful in Spain.

Leaving the cloister, you come to the diocesan museum, where the exhibits include a unique collection of tapestries owned by the cardinals of Tarragona. It is the most beautiful collection of Flemish wall hangings that exists. Its *pièce de résistance* is the *Tapiz de la Vida* dating from the late 15th c.

Nowhere else, apart from Rome itself, will you find evidence of different centuries so close together as in Tarragona. After just a few minutes' walk through the picturesque alleyways of the old town you will find yourself at the entrance to the Passeig Arqueològic, a unique promenade alongside the city wall, the latter being over 2 km long and between 3 and 10 m high. Archae- ologists still cannot agree whether the foundations of this 'cyclopean wall',

built of giant square stone blocks without any mortar, date from Iberian times or whether they are from early Roman times under the Scipios (about 200 B.C.). At various places along the promenade there are splendid views over the city, the sea and the fertile, graceful hinterland. At the end of the promenade you pass through the *Portal i Creu de Sant Antoni*, and return along streets some of which are already familiar to you to the Rambla Nova, where the many restaurants, cafés and bars invite you to take a well earned rest.

Outside the town

If your thirst for looking at antiquities is still not slaked, you should see the early Christian burial site (necropolis) near

El Arc de Berà, Tarragona

Interior of monastery, Poblet

the main road to Tortosa. It was formed between the 3rd and 5th c., and contains, in addition to some 2000 graves, richly decorated sarcophagi, mosaics, gravestones and urns. (Closed between 1 and 3 p.m.)

Also outside the town, by the side of the motorway to Barcelona, stands the

aqueduct (popularly known as *Pont del Diable*, or Devil's Bridge), dating from the time of the Emperor Trajan, about A.D. 100. The upper row of arches is 217 m long. The aqueduct supplied the town with water from the Riu Gaià. At one time the whole system extended for 35 km.

🚌 Santes Creus

An excursion into the Tarragona hinterland can be combined with a visit to the monastery of *Santes Creus* (about 30 km north-east of Tarragona). The former Cistercian monastery, standing in a valley near the Riu Gaià, was founded by Count Ramón Berenguer IV of Aragón in the year 1157. In the Middle Ages it was, except for Montserrat and Poblet, the most important monastery in Catalonia, and it contains the graves of various kings of Aragón. Typical of the time, because they were necessary, are the defensive walls. The structure is an impressive example of sometimes grandiose, sometimes more intimate Romanesque and Gothic architecture, with rich cloisters, peaceful courtyards, imposing pillars and quiet cells.

Olives and vines at Poblet

Decoration at Santes Creus

Monasterio de Santes Creus

Useful things to know...

Before you go

Climate

Catalonia has a Mediterranean climate, while south of Barcelona it is sub-tropical. In the province of Girona you can expect temperatures of 0° to 30° and water temperatures of 11° to 23°. Places north of Cap de Begur must expect to be hit occasionally by the Tramontana, a strong wind from the north, which those indulging in water-sports would do well not to underestimate.

The best time to travel is June to September. If it is too early or too late in the year to bathe on the Costa Brava, you can still expect mild air and water temperatures south of Barcelona on the Costa Daurada.

What to take

In the larger holiday resorts on the coast, in Barcelona in particular, you can, of course, find just about everything you would normally need on holiday. Good sun-glasses are indispensable. These can be bought locally but if you need special glasses or a particular suntan lotion, etc., it is advisable to take these with you. On the other hand beach-shoes, canvas sailing-shoes, straw hats and other beach requirements are so easily and cheaply available that it is not worth while taking them. Photographers who insist on top-quality film should stock up at home. The light conditions will almost certainly mean that you will need a lens-hood and filters. It is always useful to take some reading matter with you.

First-aid kit. There are *farmacias* (chemists) in all the larger towns where you can obtain many preparations. However, you would be well advised to have your own first-aid kit with you.

Certainly you should take any medicines which have been prescribed for you or which you regularly use at home, plus remedies for stomach and digestive upsets, headaches and colds (which can strike at any time), and a supply of pain killers.

For minor injuries pack an elastic bandage, plasters, an antiseptic in a well sealed bottle and anti-inflammatory cream. If your eyes are sensitive to light or strain pack some eye-drops or ointment. Take some foot powder to help prevent infection if walking barefoot.

Insurance

As a member of the EC, Spain has a reciprocal agreement with other EC countries under which free medical treatment can be obtained for those entitled to it in their own country. To obtain this benefit, it is essential for a UK national to be in possession of form E.111, obtainable from the DSS; an application form is available at main post offices.

In addition, however, it cannot be emphasised too strongly that you should take out a holiday insurance with a reputable company. Most tour operators will include this as part of the overall package, or you may prefer to make your own arrangements. While the precise scope of the cover may vary slightly, it will normally provide protection against personal accident, medical expenses, loss or damage to personal baggage, loss of money and passport, cancellation or curtailment, personal liability, etc.

Getting to the Costa Brava

By air: Most visitors to Spain travel by air. There are regular services from London, with connecting flights from principal British and Irish airports, to the

International airport of Barcelona. Many charter flights also operate, some of which use the regional airport of Girona.

By rail: The journey from London to Barcelona takes about 22 hours. You can leave London in the morning, change in Paris to the Barcelona Talgo train and arrive in Girona at 7.20 and Barcelona at about 8.30 the following morning. Sleepers and couchettes are available.

By road: It is a very long way from Great Britain to the Costa Brava — more than 1300 km — and it is advisable to allow two or three days for the journey. The time spent behind the wheel, however, can be shortened by making use of one of the motorail services through France.

Immigration and Customs Regulations

A British Visitor's Passport (valid for one year) is sufficient for holidays of up to three months. If you are staying longer a full passport and a visa are required.

Customs. Following the entry of Spain into the EC, British visitors now enjoy the more generous EC customs allowances: 300 cigarettes or 75 cigars or 400 grammes of tobacco; 1.5 litres of spirits (over 22% alcohol) or 3 litres of sparkling or fortified wine; and 4 litres of other wine. Other goods and souvenirs up to a value of £28 are also allowed in duty free. These allowances also apply on return to Great Britain.

During your stay

Currency

The unit of currency is the peseta, abbreviated to Pta. or Pts. in the plural. There are coins for 1, 2, 5, 10, 25, 50, 100 and 500 Pts. and notes of 100, 200, 500, 1000, 2000, 5000 and 10,000 Pts. At the present time £1 = 180 Pts. but, of course, this fluctuates and it is worth comparing the rates when you exchange money. Do not carry around large sums

of cash; take a few pesetas for your outward journey, a little sterling for your return and take the rest in traveller's cheques. Eurocheques are becoming more widely accepted and facilities now exist for holidaymakers to cash personal cheques if backed by a bank Eurocheque card. A sign reading *telebanco más proxima,* usually displayed at the entrance or in the window of those banks linked to the system, will tell you the whereabouts of the nearest cash-dispenser. Access, Visa and other credit cards are now widely accepted in Spain.

Electricity

Occasionally you may come across 100–125 volts, but most of the country has now been converted to 220 volts A.C. For safety's sake enquire before using any appliance. You will need to take a Continental adaptor with you.

Opening times

Banks are normally open from 9 a.m. until 2 p.m. (1 p.m. on Saturdays).

Government offices: Even the public authorities do not deny themselves the siesta; it applies to them as well! However, you will always find somebody there between 9 a.m. and midday. Some offices also open for part of the afternoon, but it is best to enquire beforehand. Your hotel reception will no doubt be able to find details of afternoon opening times for you.

Museums: Unfortunately there are no standard opening times for the museums in this area, so it is impossible to generalise. However, one time is common to all of them: you will always find the doors open between 10 a.m. and 12.30 p.m. on weekdays. Many are also open between 4 and 6 p.m. but it is best to enquire beforehand. Sundays and Public Holidays also vary — a lot of museums open, but others treat these as rest days. All museums are closed on Mondays.

Shops: The traditional siesta after lunch determines the way business is carried on in Spain and that explains what seem to us strange opening times — 9 a.m. to 1 p.m. and 5 to 8 p.m. However, many shops, especially those in the large tourist resorts which sell souvenirs and newspapers, stay open until midnight.

Post and Telephone

Post: The Post offices (*correos*) are open from 9 a.m. to 2 p.m. and in the afternoon for the sale of stamps only. These may also be obtained from any tobacconist (*estanco*). These shops are marked with either the national colours of red-yellow-red, or a stylised 'T' on a tobacco leaf. Any post office will accept items sent 'poste restante' (*lista de correos*).

The postal charge for a letter up to 20 grammes to Europe or the UK is at present 40 Pts., and it costs 30 Pts. for a postcard.

Telephone: The telephone service is independent of the post office. There are telephone offices (*telefónica* or *locutorio público*) in the provincial capitals and tourist resorts. In almost every town you will find telephone boxes from which you can make international calls direct using 25 and 100 Pts. coins; dial the international code 07, wait for the second dialling tone and then dial 44 for Great Britain. A local call from a telephone box will cost 10 Pts. for 3 minutes. To continue put in a further 5 Pts. coin.

Street and place names

In the last few years all street and place names (on maps as well as on road signs) have been changed into Catalan. Therefore they are often different from those that appear on older maps. In this guide we have used Catalan for all place names (see also page 94).

Tipping

Tips make friends, but only if they come from the heart! That may seem to be asking a lot, but the Spaniards are rather different from other Mediterranean peoples in this matter — prouder, if you like. In the hotel, if you are staying a longish time, it is worth while giving the waiters and room maids a tip every week. Don't be mean; unless you have any complaints, 200–400 Pts. is not too much. Taxi drivers, hair dressers, porters and shoe-shine boys also expect a tip.

Traffic regulations

Remember to drive on the right and

Montserrat Monastery

overtake on the left, and to give way to traffic coming from the right. Be extra careful when passing through small villages where the people might not be used to traffic.

Speed limits in Spain are: motorways 120 km p.h. (75 m.p.h.); other main roads 100 km p.h. (60 m.p.h.) or 90 km p.h. (55 m.p.h.); in towns and built-up areas 60 km p.h. (36 m.p.h.).

Transport in the area

Buses

Travelling by public transport is usually cheaper in Spain than in the UK. Admittedly, on the country routes it is not always very comfortable, but it can be very convivial! Sometimes a bus journey provides the best opportunity of coming into close contact with the local inhabitants. Timetables are displayed in the regional tourist offices.

A public service bus runs several times a day between most places on the Costa Brava and Barcelona. For places north of Palafrugell it is advisable to take the bus as far as Girona or Figueres and then continue by train to Barcelona.

Car hire

There are car-hire firms in all the main towns and tourist resorts. As well as SEAT models, which are the most common in Spain, there are also French, American and German makes available. It is very important that, whatever firm you go to, you make sure that fully comprehensive insurance cover is included. To hire a car you must be over 21 and in possession of a full driving licence.

The main arterial roads of Catalonia are very busy, especially in the holiday season. Lorry drivers will often wave you on if it is safe to overtake. The side roads are usually quiet but with many bends and hills.

Railways

The Spanish railway system, RENFE, is very good but not very widely developed and the trains are sometimes slow. The cost of travel is usually cheaper than in the UK.

Taxis

Fares are reasonable but there are three tariffs depending on the zone and the time of day. If the taxi has a meter make sure that it is working before you start on your journey. For cross-country trips you should come to an agreement with the driver beforehand.

Important addresses

Diplomatic and Consular Offices

In U.K.

Spanish Embassy
24 Belgrave Square
London SW1X 8QA; tel. (01) 235 5555.

In Spain

British Embassy
Calle de Fernando el Santo 16,
Madrid 4; tel. 4 19 02 00.

British Consulate
Avinguda Diagonal 477,
Edificio Torre de Barcelona, 13th floor,
Barcelona; tel. 3 22 21 51.

Tourist Information Offices

In UK

Spanish National Tourist Office
57-58 St James Street
London SW1A 1LD; tel. (01) 499 0901.

In Spain

Gran Via de les Corts Catalanes 658,
Barcelona; tel. 3 01 74 43.

Carrer Ciutadans 12,
Girona; tel. 20 16 94.

You will also find Tourist Information Offices, providing local information, in all the major towns and holiday resorts.

Safety abroad

It is unfortunately true that petty crime, in the form of stealing from cars, picking of pockets, snatching of handbags and other forms of pilfering, is today a regrettable fact of life in the majority of countries.

When on holiday you should take all possible steps to avoid becoming a victim of the opportunist thief. Insurance of money and baggage is strongly recommended. Do not carry large sums of money or valuables on your person. These can usually be deposited in a safe in your hotel. Women should not wear valuable jewellery and handbags should be carried on the inside arm when walking on the pavement; and men should not carry a wallet in a hip pocket.

Do not leave any valuables on view in a car. Cars are very rarely stolen — they are only relieved of their contents. Do not park at night in an unlit street but look for a busy spot, or best of all put the car in a secure car park or garage.

Should you run into difficulties go to the *Comisaría de Policía* in the city (not to the Policía Municipal) or to the *Guardia Civil* if you are in the country.

Useful words and phrases

Although English is widely understood in those parts of Spain which are frequented by tourists, the visitor will undoubtedly find a few words and phrases of Spanish very useful. In general pronunciation is not too difficult; ñ sounds very like the ni in onion; x, and c before e and i, are usually lisped; a final d generally becomes th (as in thin) and a medial d like th in the. Pronounce ll as if it were ly — or in some places y.

A word ending in a vowel or in n or s is normally stressed on the last syllable but one; a word ending in any other consonant on the final syllable. Any exceptions bear an acute accent on the stressed syllable.

please	¡ por favor !	
thank you (very much)	¡ (muchas) gracias !	
yes / no	si / no	
excuse me	¡ con permiso !	
do you speak English ?	¿ Habla Usted inglés ?	
I do not understand	No entiendo	
good morning	¡ Buenos dias !	
good afternoon	¡ Buenas tardes !	
good night	¡ Buenas noches !	
goodbye	¡ Adiós !	
how much is (it)?	¿ Qué precio tiene ?	
I should like	Quisiera	
a room with private bath	un habitación con baño	
the bill, please!	¡ la cuenta (la nota) por favor !	
everything included	todo incluido	
when is it open ?	¿ A qué hora está abierto ?	
when is it shut ?	¿ A qué hora se cierra ?	
where is ..... Street ?	¿ Dónde está la Calle......?	
the road to.... ?	el camino para ..... ?	
how far ?	¿ Qué distancia ?	
to the left / right	a la izquierda / derecha	
straight on	siempre derecho	
post office	correo	
railway station	estación	
Town Hall	Ayuntamiento	
exchange office	cambio	
police station	comisaría	
public telephone	teléfono público	0 cero
Tourist Information Office	Oficina de Información de Turismo	1 un(o)
doctor	médico	2 dos
chemist	farmacia	3 tres
toilet	retrete	4 cuatro
ladies	señoras	5 cinco
gentlemen	señores	6 seis
engaged	ocupado	7 siete
free	libre	8 ocho
entrance	entrada	9 nueve
exit	salida	10 diez
today / tomorrow	hoy / mañana	11 once
Sunday / Monday	domingo / lunes	12 doce
Tuesday / Wednesday	martes / miércoles	20 veinte
Thursday / Friday	jueves / viernes	50 cincuenta
Saturday / holiday	sábado / día festivo	100 ciento

Spanish and Catalan place names

Spanish	Catalan
Ampurdán	Empordà
Ampurias	Empúries
Bagur	Begur
Cabo Creus	Cap de Creus
Cabo de San Sebastian	Cap de Sant Sebastià
Cabo Norfeo	Cap Norfeu
Caldas del Estrad	Caldas d'Estrac (Caldetes)
Castillo d'Aro	Castell d'Aro
Condado de San Jorge	Comtat de Sant Jordí
Costa Dorada	Costa Daurada
Estartít	L'Estartit
Figueras	Figueres
Gerona	Girona
Islas Medes	Illes Medes
La Escala	L'Escala
Llafranch	Llafranc
Llansá	Llançà
Maresma	Maresme
Masnou	El Masnou
Mongat	Montgat
Panadés	Penedès
Planes	Blanes
Playa d'Aro	Platja d'Aro
Playa de Canyellas	Platja de Canyelles
Playa de Fanals	Platja de Fanals
Playa de Gava	Platja de Gava
Playa de Pals	Platja de Pals
Playa San Pol	Platja Sant Pol
Port Bou	Portbou
Port-Lligat	Portlligat
Puerto de la Selva	El Port de la Selva
Rosas	Roses
San Antoni de Calonge	Sant Antoni de Calonge
San Felíu	Sant Feliu
San Martín de Ampurias	Sant Martí d'Empúries
San Pedro	Sant Pere
San Salvador	Sant Salvador
Santas Créus	Santes Creus
Villanueva y Geltrú	Vilanova i la Geltrú.

Index

Calle Fernando, Barcelona

Original German text: Hans Eckart Rübesamen. English translation: David Cocking. Cartography: Gert Oberländer. Illustrations: Spanish National Tourist Office, London; Travel Trade Photography (pages 5, 10, 51); Feature-Pix (page 59); Patronat De Turisme, Costa Brava, Girona (page 55); Casa Del Turisme, Calella (page 60).

Series Editor — English edition: Alec Court.

The publishers have made every endeavour to ensure the accuracy of this publication but can accept no responsibility for any errors or omissions. They would, however, appreciate notification of any inaccuracies to correct future editions.

Printed in Italy

ISBN 0-7117-0467-8